INSIGHT POCKET GUIDE

Mallorca

Discovery CHANNEL

APA PUBLICATIONS
Part of the Langenscheidt Publishing Group

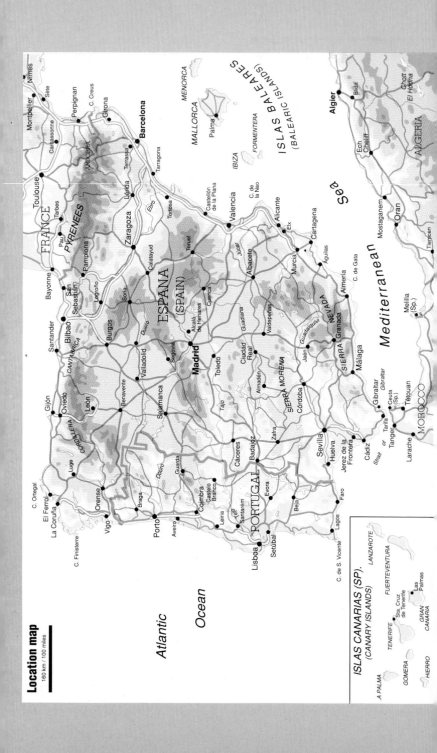

Location map

160 km / 100 miles

Welcome!

This guidebook combines the interests and enthusiasms of two of the world's best-known information providers: Insight Guides, who have set the standard for visual travel guides since 1970, and Discovery Channel, the world's premier source of non-fiction television programming.

The main aim of this guide is to take you off the beaten track (though just for fun, we've included the best of what the 'beaten track' has to offer as well) with a choice of carefully crafted itineraries, designed by Insight Guides' correspondents on Mallorca, Don Murray and Ana Pascual. The tours are divided into three sections. The first, Day Itineraries, gives you the essential flavour of Mallorca in just five days – guiding you to its loveliest mountain villages, its finest views, its most interesting architecture, and, of course, the best of its superb beaches. The second section, Pick & Mix, focuses on other interesting aspects of the island, and the third, Excursions, offers three itineraries that can be linked as a three-day tour. In addition, there are sections on history and culture, nightlife, eating out, shopping, festivals and practical information.

Don Murray and **Ana Pascual** have lived on Mallorca for many years. Between them, they have written more than a dozen books and several hundred articles on the island. Their chief advice to visitors is to leave their car as often as possible and enjoy the island on foot, leaving plenty of time for long lazy lunches and soaking up the sun.

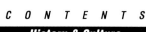

C O N T E N T S

History & Culture

From the civilising influences of the Romans and the
Moors to the revolutionary effects of modern tourism
– an account of the people and issues that have
shaped Mallorca..**10–16**

Mallorca's Highlights

**These five full-day itineraries concentrate on
Mallorca's principal sights and beauty spots.**

Day 1 Palma Historica is a tour of *Palma*'s old
quarter, discovering its splendid architecture, from
Arab baths to Gothic palaces and baroque churches.............**22**

Day 2 Sóller, Deià and Valldemossa is a winding
drive north of Palma to *Sóller*, a town known for its
modernist architecture, and then along the coast to the
hamlet of *Lluc-Alcari*, where Robert Graves is buried,
and then to *Valldemossa*...**29**

Day 3 Faro Formentor journeys across the island
to its northernmost point at *Cap de Formentor*. Sights
on the way include the caves of *Campanet*, *Pollença*
and the Roman ruins in *Alcúdia*...**33**

Day 4: Andratx and Banyalbufa heads west along
the PM1 to *Andrat x* and then north to *Banyalbufa*,
passing busy resorts, quiet villages and pretty bays..............**37**

Day 5 Inca and Lluc combines a visit to *Inca*, a
town known for its leather, with a drive through
spectacular scenery to *Lluc*, the religious centre of
Mallorca..**41**

Pick & Mix Itineraries

**The following nine itineraries are designed to suit a
range of time frames and tastes.**

1 Hermitages focuses on some of Mallorca's many
religious sanctuaries, including the hill-top hermitage
of *Sant Salvador* and *Cura*, with its *Museum and
Gramática of Ramón Llull*, a 13th-century religious
philosopher..**44**

2 Mountain Passage is a picturesque drive
through the *Serra de Tramuntana*, stopping at the
Monasteri de Nostra Senyora de Lluc, where you can
hear the Blauets choir...**47**

3 Mallorca's Interior explores characterful
villages, stopping to sample local wines along the way........**51**

4 Palma's Museums offers a choice of five
museums where you can while away a morning,
including the *Palau de l'Almudaina* and the *Pueblo
Español*...**55**

*Pages 2/3:
Montieri, on
Mallorca's
central plain*

5 Valldemossa pays a visit to a town that has been
the summer residence for many famous people,
including Frederick Chopin and George Sand **57**

6 Train from Palma to Sóller takes a ride on an
antique train to *Sóller*..**59**

7 Windmills of the Pla de Palma heads east into
windmill country and then south to *Cap Blanc* **62**

8 Serra de Tramuntana Foothills explores one of
the least known areas of Mallorca **65**

9 Galilea visits a 13th-century monastery and the
Italian-style house-museum of *Sa Granja*.............................. **68**

Excursions

These three excursions can either be followed
individually or strung together as a three-day tour.

10 Palma to Alcúdia focuses on the walled city of
Alcúdia, Pollentia and the *Sanctuary of Sant Sebastià*.
An overnight stop is suggested in *Cala Ratjada*....................**71**

11 The Northeast Coast drives south along the
coast, visiting the *Gardens of Torre Cega*, the *Castell
de Capdepera*, the *Coves d'Artá* and *Porto Cristo*..................**74**

12 The Southeast Coast is a drive between *Porto
Cristo* and *Santanyí* stopping at the *Coves del Drac,
Porto Colom, S'Horta* and *Porto Petro*....................................**77**

*Pages 8/9:
on the beach*

Nightlife, Dining Experiences & Shopping

Tips on where to stay up late, where to dine and what
to buy in Palma **80–94**

Calendar of Events

A month by month guide to the island's main festivals **96–9**

Practical Information

All the background information you may need for your
stay, including a list of recommended hotels **100–109**

Maps

Spain	.4	*Santa María del Camí*	.51
Mallorca Routes	.10–21	*Sineu*	.53
Palma de Mallorca	.24	*Petra*	.54
Sóller	.29	*Alcúdia*	.71
Valldemossa	.32	*Porto Cristo*	.75
Pollença	.34		

Index and Credits 110–19

Island of the Calm

It may be said that the history of Mallorca is as long as its coastline. Were it not for the 5,547km (3,439 miles) of coast, we can be very sure that the island's past, present and future would be very different. Mallorca, like other major islands of the Mediterranean, has attracted a cornucopia of conquerors, invaders, settlers and tourists, who have all contributed to its richness and vital history.

The formation of the Balearic islands is assumed to have taken place around 150 million years ago. At first, Mallorca was joined to the peninsula as an underwater island. One hundred and forty-nine million years later, more or less, its present configuration came into being. Scrub forests comprising pine, rosemary, wild olive, lentiscus and dwarf fan palms were the island's main vegetation. Rockrose and lavender predominated in the sierra.

The sparse vegetation supported only a few animals. The smallest were field mice and wood shrews; the largest, the civet cats. Birds, on the other hand, have always been plentiful. Even though their habitat is under constant threat, counting the migrators and a few

Palma's waterfront in the mid-17th century (Ajuntament de Palma)

indigenous species, they number today well over 2,000 species. But of all the non-human species on Mallorca, it is only the pine tree which isn't in decline. As for *homo sapiens*, the present population stands at 630,000, and is increasing at a frightening rate.

Rainfall on the island is slight, varying between 1,400mm (55in) in the mountains to only 300mm (11.8in) on the southern plain. The winds blow principally during the winter and spring, when they are predominantly out of the north (the Tramuntana) and the

southwest (the Llebeix). The southeast Sirocco brings with it red sand from the deserts of Africa which, if nothing else, seriously irritates the island's clean-car owners.

For most Mallorcans, history didn't really begin until the Catalans retook the island from the Moors in the 13th century. On the other hand, experts date the first islanders to between 1300 and 1000BC. Even though the earliest people obviously carried on primitive but active trade with others around the western Mediterranean, the quantity of arms found in their early dwellings shows that the island still had a long way to go before becoming the 'Island of the Calm'.

Because of the location of the archipelago, the Balearic islands found themselves on the great trading routes that criss-crossed the Mediterranean Sea. Eivissa (Ibiza) became an important commercial centre for first the Phoenicians, then the Carthaginian traders. While Mallorca played only a minor part in these 8th- and 7th-century BC cultures, there are references in classical texts to Mallorcan *honderos* (stone slingers) fighting for the Carthaginians in the Punic wars.

When the winners, the Romans, finally tired of the piracy that was rife in the Baleares, they organised an expedition to conquer and settle Mallorca. In 123BC Quinto Cecilio Metelo conquered the island, and for five and a half centuries Mallorca was subject to the vicissitudes of Roman history. Historians believe that at the time there were two major centres, Pollentia (beside Alcúdia) and Palma. After a few centuries more of 'ups and downs' under the successive

11

domination of the Vandals and the Byzantines, the Muslims began 200 years of attacks on the island at the beginning of the 8th century AD. In 902 the entire archipelago was annexed to the Emirate of Córdoba.

While Roman culture probably had the greatest impact on Mallorcan social patterns, the influence of the Moors was responsible for important advances in the island's agriculture, along with development of the island's crafts and commerce. It is also easy to pinpoint the Moorish contribution to the island's folklore, language and cuisine.

Jaume I, the Conqueror

It was the Mallorcan Moors' plundering of Catalan boats that finally provoked King Jaume I to plan the overthrow of the island. At the end of the year 1229, 15,000 men with 1,500 horses aboard

155 ships set sail from Salou, in Tarragona. Bloody details aside, Jaume I, the Conqueror, annexed the island to his Kingdom of Aragón. The monarch then subdivided this newly enlarged kingdom between his two sons – the younger, Jaume, got Mallorca.

Jaume II's domination of Mallorca lasted only a brief period. As an independent kingdom, from 1276 to 1344, the island lived through what the historians call a 'Golden Age'. Jaume's reign saw a flowering of the island's agriculture, industry and navigation. A number of new villages were founded, coins were minted, Bellver Castle was built. In addition, the Almudaina was transformed into a splendid Gothic palace and the building of the Convent of Sant Francesc

Ramón Llull monument, Palma

was begun. It was also the time of the Mallorcan philosopher and scientist Ramón Llull.

But the Catalans were not happy about Mallorca's independent successes. In 1344 they resorted to brute force, reincorporating the islands definitively into the Kingdom of Aragón. At the end of the 15th century, the Baleares were united with the Kingdom of Spain as part of the political union of Castile and Aragón.

During the following centuries, Mallorcan villagers were at odds with their neighbours in the city. Sometimes they displayed their rancour by bad-mouthing their foes, while at other times there was bloodshed. A series of uprisings in the 16th century were caused by popular discontent against the nobility. Meanwhile, plague was rampaging through Europe, decimating populations, including thousands of Mallorcans.

Spain's first civil war took place in the following century. Called the 'War of Succession' because it would determine who would succeed the heirless king, it had great repercussions on Mallorca. Until this point the Austrian dynasty, the Habsburgs, had allowed Mallorca a state of semi-autonomy. The possibility of a French Bourbon king acceding, with ideas of an 'absolute' monarchy, divided the population of the island to such an extent that even now historians aren't sure exactly who supported whom.

However, when, in 1700, Felipe v finally ascended to the Spanish throne, the Mallorcans gave him their approval. The Grand and General Council was replaced by an 'Audience' supervised by a Captain General of the King's troops, and the use of Castilian (the Spanish language) was made obligatory for all public and official transactions.

The next chapter in Mallorca's history was, if not fun, at least romantic. The island lived in constant fear of pirate attacks from North Africa. In response, several generations of notable Mallorcan sailors were given permission by the king to 'defend' their homeland. Needless to say, the licence – the *patente de corso* – proved enormously beneficial. The most famous of the corsairs (named after this licence) was Captain Antoni Barceló, who eventually achieved the rank of Lieutenant General of the Spanish Armada by such acts as renting ships to the navy whenever it was short of sea power.

Another famous personage from the same era was the Mallorcan missionary Fray Junípero Serra. Born in the tiny inland village of Petra, Serra travelled considerably further than Barceló. In fact, without the Mallorcan missionary, San Francisco and many other Californian cities might not exist today.

The Napoleonic wars, at the beginning of the 19th century, put a damper on the heady days of previous decades. Catalan refugees poured into Mallorca, causing both social and economic unrest among the islanders. But the same century also saw the birth of the bourgeoisie and its impulse for social change. Communications with the peninsula were installed, shipping lines to exploit trade with the Indies were established, the broad, marshy plain near Palma was pumped dry and the land reclaimed for agricultural purposes, the railway was built and a timid regionalism emerged with the renewed use of the Catalan language.

But the end of the century saw another falling of local economic fortunes. The *phylloxera* did away with the island's booming wine business and the loss of Cuba, Puerto Rico and the Philippines as colonies put an abrupt halt to much of the local shipbuilding. Many of the islanders, seeing the writing on the wall (and the lack of food in the pantry), emigrated to the peninsula and America.

The first half of the 20th century on Mallorca was dominated by two men: the politician Antoni Maura and the financier Joan March. Maura, the leader of the conservative party, spent all of his political life in Madrid, but never lost the loyal support of his fellow islanders. The life of Joan March Ordinas was the archetypal 'from rags to riches' story. Born in a Mallorcan village at a time of strong class prejudices on the part of the ruling elite, he became not only the richest man in Spain, but was thought to be the third richest man in the world (after John Paul Getty and Howard Hughes).

The Mallorcans continued into the third decade of the 20th century much as they had left the 1800s – provincial, extremely religious and politically conservative. With the governing classes firmly on the side of Francisco Franco from the very beginning, the islands saw little violence during the Spanish Civil War. During the dictatorship, the political situation in the islands was the same as that on the peninsula. It wasn't until the 1960s and the arrival of tourism that Mallorca began to dismantle its traditional way of life. In 1975, with the death of Franco, the island began the work of recovering its autonomy and cultural identity. In 1978, the new Spanish Constitution sanctioned the creation of the provincial government which exists today.

The Language Issue

Being islanders, the Mallorcans have withstood a long history of invasions by nearly everyone who could reach their coastline. As a result of these invasions they have become defensive and nationalistic. But they have also learned the advantages of trade. Trade has made them a little Phoenician themselves. They have learned to accommodate their 'visitors' while accommodating themselves.

In regard to their language, Mallorcans divide themselves into three groups: pro-Catalan, anti-Catalan and the so-called 'NO/NRs' (No Opinion/No Response). The third group is by far the largest (and obviously the most reticent). The pro-Catalanists seem to want a tight union with Catalunya, with which they share their language. Many among them spent time either in jail or in exile during the Franco years.

A few years on, most islanders are more relaxed about the whole language question. Catalan is now taught in schools, and many people speak both the Mallorcan version of Catalan and Spanish or Castilian. A new language issue is much more talked about these days. Of the six million plus tourists who visit Mallorca every year, quite a few are seduced by the island's natural beauty, mild climate and pleasant lifestyle, and decide to stay. Entire villages are taken over by German and British ex-pats, and most signs are in their languages. The Government of the Balearics has responded recently by passing a law stipulating that all signs should be first in one of the native languages, Catalan or Spanish, and only then in a foreign language.

Mallorcans are deeply divided over what to do about the exploitation of the island itself. Again, the 'silent majority' is, by far, the largest player in the arena. The others are polarised between maintaining the incredible pace of growth which Mallorca has enjoyed

over the past 20 years, or facing the reality that times are changing and the goose that laid the golden egg is being squeezed too hard. The big money is on 'continuing growth' while the ecologists are on the other side of the ring. The people who have been enticed to Mallorca are realising that those who 'sold' it to them are turning 'La Isla de la Calma' into a jungle of noise and concrete.

Hospitality

Compared to the French or the English, Mallorcans are an extremely friendly and sociable people. They are quite happy to chat with a stranger in a bar. They will greet everyone upon entering and bid everyone goodbye when they leave. They are answered by a chorus of *'Bon dia!'* from all the locals within hearing range. Most Mallorcans seem genuinely delighted if a foreigner speaks to them in either of their two languages. But to really get to know one is quite difficult.

A tradition of hospitality has developed from literally centuries of subjection to all races of invaders and, now, to tourists. But the Mallorcans expect something in return for this hospitality. They want to make a living.

Where is Mallorca going from here? For the first time in recent history almost everyone agrees that growth cannot continue at its present accelerated rate. People talk about 'high-class tourism' without mention of the areas beyond repair. And since it is far easier to build more on Mallorca than to tear down and replace existing developments, the island may end up with ghost towns bleaching in the summer sun. Our bet is that the island will go on much the way it is today. The worst of the construction will fall into disuse (and hopefully be torn down), expansion will trickle to a halt and everyone will have time to take a long hard look at the island's recent past for guidance to its future.

Historical Highlights

1300–1000 BC: Height of the Talayotic culture. Warring tribes carry on primitive trade around the eastern Mediterranean.

700–146: Baleares dominated by Phoenicians then Carthaginians.

123: Mallorca conquered by Quinto Cecilio Metelo; the Baleares join the Roman Empire. The islands are Christianised in the 2nd century AD.

426 AD: Vandals devastate the islands and persecute Christians.

534: The Christian religion is restored by the Byzantines.

707: First Muslim attack on the Baleares.

902: The Baleares are annexed to the Emirate of Córdoba.

1015: Mallorca is annexed to another Muslim 'kingdom', the 'Taifa of Denia'.

1087–1114: Mallorca becomes an independent *taifa*.

1114: A group of Pisa-Catalans manage to conquer Eivissa and Mallorca. The siege of Palma lasts eight months. After the city is defeated and sacked, the invaders go home.

1115–1203: The Almorávides, a tribe from North Africa, arrive to help the Mallorcan Muslims and stay on to occupy the island. The island experiences a period of prosperity. The Almorávides' dominion extends to all of the islands and to Tunisia and Tripolitania.

1203–29: The Baleares fall into the hands of Almohadian tribes from Algeria and Denia. Political instability allows the reconquest of Mallorca by the Catalans.

1229: Catalan King Jaume I of Aragón occupies and conquers Mallorca on 31 December, after three months of fighting.

1235–1315: Life of Mallorcan philosopher and scientist, Ramón Llull.

1276: Death of Jaume I and creation of the independent Kingdom of Mallorca ruled by Jaume II.

1285: First attempt by the Catalans to recover the Kingdom of Mallorca by force. Later expedition returned by order of the Pope. Two years later Menorca is incorporated into the Kingdom of Aragón by King Alfons III.

1291: Jaume II of Aragón returns the Baleares, including Menorca, to his uncle, Jaume II of Mallorca.

1312–24: Reign of King Sanç, son of Jaume II of Mallorca.

1324–44: Reign of King Jaume III of Mallorca, bringing economic prosperity. Palma is one of the richest cities in the Mediterranean.

1344: Troops of Pere IV of Aragón invade and reincorporate the three islands into the Kingdom of Aragón.

1349: Jaume III tries to recover the Kingdom of Mallorca and dies in the Battle of Llucmajor.

1479: Kingdom of España formed by uniting the Kingdom of Castilla and the Kingdom of Aragón, including Mallorca.

1700: Felipe de Bourbón ascends to the throne. Beginning of the War of Succession.

1715: Troops loyal to Felipe V arrive. The law of the *Nueva Planta* is decreed. Three years later the *Gran i General Consell* is dissolved.

1713–84: Life of Fray Junípero Serra, founder of the missions of California.

1785: Treaty of Algiers signed, ending piracy while establishing the Mallorcan 'corsairs'.

1808–13: The War of Independence against the invading troops of Napoleon. Many refugees arrive on Mallorca, provoking social tension.

1820–22: Massive emigration to Algeria and South America.

1837: First regular steamship line between Mallorca and the peninsula.

1879–98: The years of the 'gold fever'. Period of prosperity thanks to the wine and almond trades. Ends with arrival of the *phylloxera* and loss of Spain's last colonies.

1936–9: Spanish Civil War.

1939–75: Dictatorship of Franco.

1978: Approval of new Spanish Constitution, which opens the doorway to the creation of 'autonomies'.

1983: Approval of the Statutes of Autonomy for the Baleares; first elections held shortly thereafter.

Route map

16 km / 10 miles

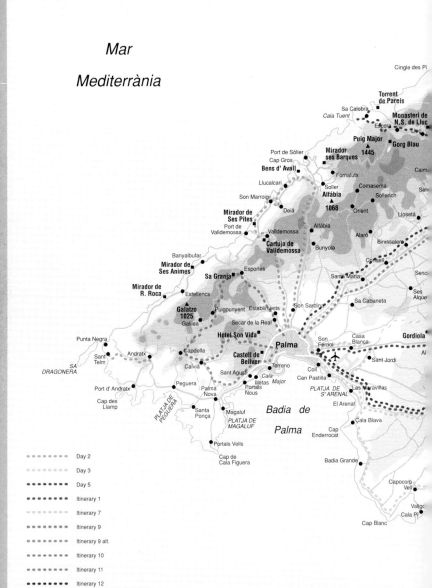

Mar

Mediterrània

Cingle des Pi

Torrent
de Pareis

Sa Calobra
Cala Tuent

Monasteri de
N.S. de Lluc

Escora

Lluc

Puig Major
1445

Gorg Blau

Port de Sóller
Cap Gros

Mirador
ses Barques

Bens d' Avall

Fornalutx

Caim

Llucalcari

Soller

Comasema

Sellerich

Alfábia

Son Marroig

Deiá

1068

Orient

Lioseta

Mirador de
Ses Pites

Alfábia

Llosetà

Port de
Valldemossa

Valldemossa

Cartuja de
Valldemossa

Bunyola

Alaró

Binissalem

Banyalbufar

Esporles

Consell

Mirador de
Ses Animes

Sa Granja

Santa Maria

Senc

Mirador de
R. Roca

Estellencs

Son Sardina

Sa Cabaneta

Ses
Alque

Galatzo
1025
Galilea

Puigpunyent

Establiments

Secar de la Real

Hotel Son Vida

Palma

Son
Ferriol

Casa
Blanca

Gordiola

Punta Negra

Andratx

Capdella

Castell de
Bellver

Sant Jordi

Al

SA
DRAGONERA

Sant
Telm

Calvia

Terreno

Coll

Cala
Major

Can Pastilla

Port d' Andratx

Peguera

Sant Agustí

Illetas
Portals
Nous

PLATJA DE
S' ARENAL

Las Maravillas

Cap des
Llamp

Palma
Nova

El Arenal

PLATJA DE
PEGUERA

Santa
Ponça

Magaluf

Badia   de

PLATJA DE
MAGALUF

Palma

Cala Blava

Portals Vells

Cap
Enderrocat

Cap de
Cala Figuera

Badia Grande

Capocorb
Vell

Vallgc
Cala Pi

Cap Blanc

- - - - - - - Day 2
- - - - - - - Day 3
●●●●●●● Day 5
●●●●●●● Itinerary 1
- - - - - - - Itinerary 7
●●●●●●● Itinerary 9
●●●●●●● Itinerary 9 alt.
●●●●●●● Itinerary 10
●●●●●●● Itinerary 11
●●●●●●● Itinerary 12

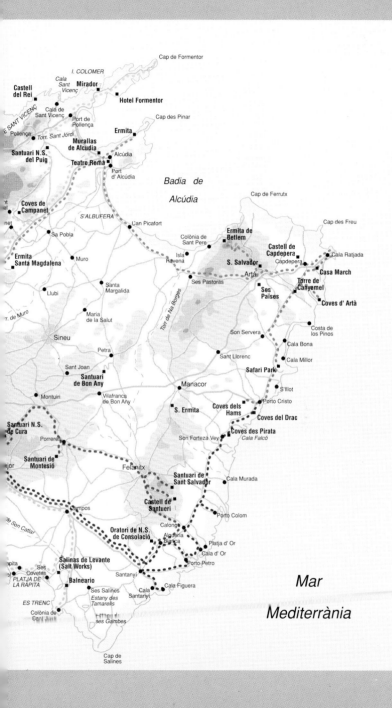

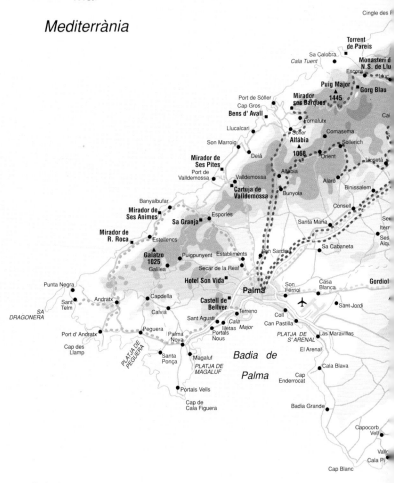

Mar

Mediterrània

Cingle des F

Torrent
de Pareis

Sa Calobra
Cala Tuent

Monasteri d
N.S. de Llu

Escorca

Lluc

Puig Major
▲1445

Gorg Blau

Port de Sóller

Mirador
ses Barques

Cap Gros

Bens d' Avall

Fornalutx

Cai

Llucalcari

Comasema

Sóller

Sollerich

Son Marroig

Alfábia
▲1068

Orient

Lloseta

Deiá

Mirador de
Ses Pites

Port de
Valldemossa

Valldemossa

Alfábia

Alaró

Binissalem

Cartuja de
Valldemossa

Bunyola

Banyalbufar

Consell

Mirador de
Ses Animes

Esporles

Sa Granja

Santa Maria

Se

Mirador de
R. Roca

Estellencs

Iterr

Ses
Alqu

Galatzo
▲1025
Galilea

Puigpunyent

Establiments

Can Sardi

Sa Cabaneta

Secar de la Real

Punta Negra

Hotel Son Vida

Palma

Son
Férriol

Casa
Blanca

Gordiol

Andratx

Capdella

Castell de
Bellver

Sant Jordi

*SA
DRAGONERA*

Sant
Telm

Calvia

Terreno

Coll

Sant Agusti

*Cala
Major*

Can Pastilla

Port d' Andratx

Peguera

Palma
Nova

Illetas

Portals
Nous

*PLATJA DE
S' ARENAL*

Las Maravillas

Cap des
Llamp

*PLATJA
DE
PEGUERA*

Santa
Ponça

Magaluf

El Arenal

Badia de

Cala Blava

*PLATJA DE
MAGALUF*

Palma

Cap
Enderrocat

Portals Vells

Cap de
Cala Figuera

Badia Grande

Capocorb
Vell

Vallo
Cala Pi

Cap Blanc

○ ○ ○ ○ ○ ○ ○	Day 4
● ● ● ● ● ● ●	Itinerary 2
○ ○ ○ ○ ○ ○ ○	Itinerary 3
○ ○ ○ ○ ○ ○ ○	Itinerary 5
● ● ● ● ● ● ●	Itinerary 8

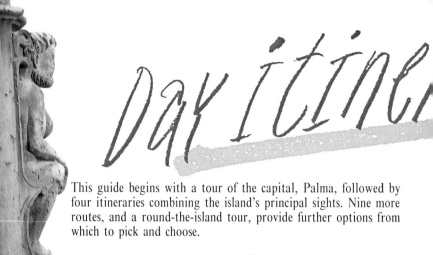

This guide begins with a tour of the capital, Palma, followed by four itineraries combining the island's principal sights. Nine more routes, and a round-the-island tour, provide further options from which to pick and choose.

Day 1

Palma Historica

A guided walking tour combining modern art, Arab baths, ancient cloisters, hot chocolate in an 18th-century café, a walk among the flower sellers, a langosta in Bar Bosch, ancient shipyards and a king's garden.

Start at the **Parc del Mar**, built in the mid-1980s, a home to a collection of modern sculptures, as well as a gigantic mural by Joan Miró. From the park you get an overall view of the **Casc Antic** (the ancient centre) and the **17th and 18th-century walls** which enclose the city, more or less following earlier ones dating back to Arab times.

Cathedral viewed from Parc del Mar

City Hall façade

Enter through the walls by way of the **Porta de la Portella**, which is near the right-hand edge of the lake. On the left is the late 17th-century **Ca la Torre**, today the **Col.legi d'Arquitectes**. Next to it is the baroque doorway to the **Posada de Cartoixa**. At the first corner are the 17th-century façade and balcony of **Can Formiguera**, home of the legendary Comte Mal – or 'Bad Count'. Turning right, follow **carrer Serra** around to the left until it passes under a small bridge. The **Banys Arabs** (Arab Baths) are found at No 7. They date back to the times of the Walis (the Arab governors), during the 9th and 10th centuries.

At the next corner take a hard right and follow this short street till it enters the patio of the **Convent de Santa Clara**. Founded by King Jaume I in 1256, the accompanying church was built in the 1600s. Turn back onto carrer de Santa Clara, continue briefly on carrer de Pont i Vich, and turn right at carrer de Montesió. At No 6 is **Can Malonda**, also dating from the 17th century. In front of the baroque façade of the **Church of Montesió** is the 18th-century house of the **Baró (Baron) de Pinopar**.

Enter the carrer de la Criança beside the house and follow it to the end before turning left on carrer del Sol. The city's most important Renaissance façade, that of the **Casa del Marquäs de Palmer,** is at No 7. **Casa Juliá**, at No 3, has an interesting example of *arte mudéjar* on the ceiling of the entrance.

Turn right onto carrer de Pare Nadal and then right again into the **Plaça de Sant Francesc**. Immediately to your right is the outstanding patio of **Can Moragues**, dating from the 18th century. On the opposite side of the square, to the right of the church, is the entry to the **Cloister of the Convent of Sant Francesc**. Built in the 14th century, it embodies architectural elements added through the 16th century. The church, a Gothic structure with a baroque façade, may be entered from within the cloister. Near the church's main doorway is a statue of Mallorcan missionary Fray Junípero

Palma de Mallorca

160 m / 175 yards

1 Ca la Torre (College of Architects)
2 Banys Arabs (Arab baths)
3 Convent de Santa Clara
4 Church of the Montesio
5 Casa del Marquès de Palmer
6 Cloister of the Convent of Sant Francesc
7 Can Vivot
8 Can Joan de S'Aigua
9 Church of Santa Eulália
10 Can Oleza
11 House of the poet Guillem Colom
12 Arc de l'Almudaina
13 Can Oleo
14 Consell Insular de Mallorca
15 Plaça Cort
16 Ajuntament (City Hall)
17 Can Rei
18 Almacenes Aguila
19 Plaça Major
20 Headquarters of the March Foundation
21 Church of Sant Antoniet
22 Church of Santa Catalina
23 Plaça d'Espanya
24 La Rambla
25 Teatre Principal
26 Gran Hotel
27 Can Berga (Justice Palace)
28 Casa Casasayas
    and Pensión Menorquina
29 Círculo de Bellas Artes
30 Bar Bosch
31 Plaça Juan Carlos I
32 Can Sollerich
33 Oratori de Sant Feliu
34 Ses Carasses
35 Can Montenegro
36 Cal Capità Flexes
37 Can Llull
38 Plaça Drassanes (Atarazanas)
39 Can Chacón
40 Consulat Mar
41 La Llotja (la Lonja)
42 Monument to Ramon Llull
43 S'Hort del Rei
44 Palau March
45 Seu (Cathedral)
46 Palau de l'Almudaina
47 Gothic arch and pond
ⓘ Tourist Information
ⓣ Public Telephone Office
Ⓖ Petrol Station

Serra, founder of California (see *Pick and Mix*, Route 3). Carrer de Can Troncoso skirts the church until you turn onto carrer de Zavellá. At No 15 is the Gothic **Can Cal.lar del Llorer**. At No 4, **Can Vivot** has the city's most important patio, in the baroque style, dating from the 18th century. It is still home to the Count and Countess of Savellá. Opposite, at No 13, look into the restored 17th-century baroque entranceway of the earlier Gothic **Can Savellá**.

One block to the left, on carrer de Sanç, is the oldest café in the city, **Can Joan de S'Aigua**. Today specialising in Mallorcan hot chocolate, almond ice cream and Mallorcan pastries, it opened in the 18th century selling drinks chilled with snow brought down from the mountains.

Return to carrer Fiol, turn left and continue past the church to **Plaça de Santa Eulália**. The Gothic church is open in the mornings. Leaving the square by way of carrer de'n Morey, you will find **Can Oleza** at No 9, with one of the finest examples of Mallorcan-style patios of the 18th century. The façade is 16th-century Renaissance. At the next corner turn right onto carrer de Pere Nolasco, which runs along the front of the **Gardens of the Bishop's Palace**, then turn right onto carrer de Zanglada. The patio of the house of Mallorcan poet Guillem Colom, at No 4, contains interesting ironwork around the well. The patio itself is late-18th century baroque.

Where the street ends at carrer de l'Almudaina, look right. The **Arc de l'Almudaina** is generally thought to be Arab, but some experts believe it dates further back, to Roman times. Continuing left along the same street, both the Gothic 13th-century **Can Bordils** (No 9) and its 17th-century next-door neighbour, **Can Oms** (at No 7) are interesting public buildings which may be entered during office hours. **Can Oleo** is one of the best medieval houses in the city and may soon be opened to the public.

Turning right onto carrer Palau Reial, you will pass the towered neo-Gothic headquarters of the century-old **Consell Insular de Mallorca** (the island government) and enter into the **Plaça Cort**, which has been the hub of city life since the 13th century. The present **Ajuntament** (city hall) was built in the 17th century and is in the baroque style. You may enter the street level hallway, where you will see the elegant imperial staircase and a pair of ceremonial Mallorcan *gigants* of *papier-mâché*.

From the square, continue along carrer de'n Colòn, on which are two of the city's best examples of Modernist architecture. Grabbing most of the attention is the colourfully tiled **Can Rei** (corner of carrer Bolseria) with its grotesque frowning window box. Next door stands the eclectic work of local architect Gaspar Bennàssar, **Almacenes Aguila**. Both buildings date from the early years of the 20th century.

The archways lead into the **Plaça Major**. Built at the beginning of the 19th century on the site of the Inquisition building, it was renovated in 1951. On Monday, Friday and Saturday mornings, it is the site of a crafts market. Straight through the square on carrer de Sant Miquel you will find an early 20th-century building, the **Headquarters of the March Foundation**, which is open as a cultural centre and art gallery. Further along on the same side is the **Church of Sant Miquel**, at No 21, on the site of a mosque. On the other side, at No 32, are the **Church and Cloister of Sant Antoniet**. Built in the 18th century in late baroque style, the cloister is often the site of exhibitions ranging from displays of Japanese Bonsai trees to anti-nuclear protest material.

Continuing along carrer Sant Miquel, pass the **Church of Santa Catalina**, turn right and enter **Plaça d'Espanya**. In the centre is a monument to 'Jaume I, Conqueridor de Mallorca'. Other notable structures are the eclectic buildings of the Sóller train station on the far side of the **Avinguda Joan March Ordinas** and the two corner buildings, which also display eclectic Modernist touches. The **café 1916** is recommended for a light lunch. If you're on time, **Foto Lacor** is a good place to leave your films for quick processing.

Descend carrer d'es Olmos till it intersects **La Rambla**. This tree-lined avenue was, until the 17th century, the watercourse through Palma. Walking down among the myriad flower stalls you may catch sight, on the right-hand side, of a beautifully restored rose-coloured façade at No 9. The brace of Roman centurions at the end of the promenade date from the time of Franco. Turning right, you are confronted by the 19th-century Classicist façade of the

La Rambla

Teatre Principal, which hosts plays and concerts from April through to the end of June.

Immediately to the left, on carrer Uniò, is the **Centro Cultural de la Caixa de Barcelona**, housed in the recently restored **Gran Hotel**, a magnificent art nouveau structure built in 1902 by Catalan architect Doménech i Montaner. On the opposite side of the road is the **Palau de Justicia**, in **Can Berga**, a seignorial house dating from the 18th century. Next door sit the twin Modernist buildings of **Casa Casasayas** and **Pensión Menorquina**, built in 1910 and 1911 respectively. Further along on the right-hand side is the 18th-century **Círculo de Bellas Artes**, which often houses exhibitions.

Stop for coffee at the **Bar Bosch**, in the **Plaça Juan Carles I**. It also serves its own variety of sandwiches in rolls called *langostas*

Interior of the Círculo de Bellas Artes

(lobsters). From the terrace in front of the café you can see the arched loggia and restored details of the façade of the 18th-century palace **Can Sollerich**. The building, which is owned by City Hall, holds regular art exhibitions. The entrance can be found at **carrer Sant Gaiet 10**.

Follow the **Passeig des Born**, the wide promenade leading in the direction of the port. Originally a long finger-like inlet leading from the sea, it was filled in the 17th century, to be used as a place in which to hold popular festivals, including jousting. At the corner of carrer Sant Feliu, turn right. Passing the 18th-century seignorial mansion of **Can Quint** (above Restaurante Antonios) you soon encounter the tiny **Oratori de Sant Feliu**. The small chapel itself is 13th-century Gothic, while the façade, on carrer Gaietá, is Renaissance. A few metres further along is a design school housed in **Ses Carasses**. The inscription above the ornate doorway makes reference to the builder – an Italian merchant of the 17th century.

Backing up a few paces, turn left into carrer Montenegro. On the right is the baroque façade of **Can Montenegro**, which belonged to one of the most powerful families in the city. The large plaque on the front refers to a member of the family, who was Grand Master of the Order of Malta. Turning right into carrer Glória you arrive, at the end, between two interesting houses. On the left is the enormous **Cal Capitá Flexes** built by a 'corsair' who became incredibly rich during the 17th century. In front, and on the opposite side of Glória, is the patio opening to **Can Llull**, a tasteful restoration of the 18th-century house.

Going down the small hill you arrive at the chaotic **Plaça Drassanes (Plaza Atarazanas)**. It was the site of Mallorca's most important shipyard from the 13th to the beginning of the 19th century. In the centre is a statue of the famous Mallorcan sailor Jaume Ferrer. Leaving the square by carrer Consulat, you see above to the right **Can Chacón** and to the left the **Consulat del Mar**. The latter, built in the 17th century as a court concerned with maritime affairs, has been the seat of the provincial government – the Govern Balear – since 1983.

Continuing past the flags and cannons in front of the building, along **Passeig**, you come next to the antique **La Llotja**, which was built to house the 'College of the Merchants' in the 15th century. It was built in the Gothic style by Guillem Sagrera. Today it is used by the provincial government and is open only when there is an exhibition.

On the right, beside the main road, is the prominent statue of the 13th-century Mallorcan philosopher and scientist, **Ramon Llull**. The pedestal dedication is in Catalan, Arabic and Latin, recalling his contributions in all three languages. Crossing the **Avinguda**

Façade of the Cathedral (Seu)

Antoni Maura, named after a Mallorcan politician of the early 1900s, you will find the **S'Hort del Rei** (the Garden of the King). Originally a garden associated with the **Almudaina castle** above, it was converted for public use only a few years ago. It contains several modern sculptures as well as a bronze Mallorcan *hondero* (the early sling throwers).

At the upper end of the garden, near the egg-shaped sculpture by Joan Miró, are the stairs leading up to the Cathedral. The building on the left as you climb is the **Palau March**. It was built by Mallorcan financier Joan March in the 1940s, when he was reputed to be the third richest man in the world. On the ground level is the entrance to the March Library, the most important private library on the island. Directly in front, at the top of the stairs, is the 16th-century house of **L'Ardiacanat**.

Turn right and enter the **Plaça de l'Almoina**. Before entering the Cathedral you will see on the left a Mannerist façade with interesting details from the 17th century.

The cloister and the museum of the Cathedral are entered by way of the Gothic **Casa de l'Almoina**, which was, in times gone by, a charity house. The Cathedral (**Seu**) was begun in the 14th century and finished in the 16th, except for the main façade, which was finally completed in neo-Gothic style in the 19th century. Several styles are present, including 20th-century Modernist touches added by Antoni Gaudí between 1902 and 1914. Half of the 87 windows are cemented over. There are seven rose windows, the biggest of which has a diameter of 12.5m (41ft).

Across the square from the Cathedral is the **Palau de l'Almudaina**. This building has always been used as the centre of government for the island. It was the residence of the Muslim 'Walis' and later the kings of Mallorca. It is a typical Gothic palace of medieval date. Today the palace is part of the National Royal Patrimony and, since 1985, has been the official residence of the King of Spain when he is staying in Mallorca.

To end this tour walk down the stairs between the Cathedral and the Almudaina. Turn right at the wall. On the right you will pass a large Gothic arch and a pond before you reach the next set of steps. The archway, the **Arc de la Drassana Reial**, dates back to Arab times, when it was the entrance to the royal shipyards beside the palace.

By following the steps for a few more metres you will return to the Parc del Mar and the end of this itinerary.

Sóller, Deià and Valldemossa

Road with 58 hairpin bends; Modernist architecture in Sóller; lunch at Bens D'Avall; the grave of Robert Graves; the home of an archduke.

Leaving Palma by way of carrer 31 de Desembre and highway C-711, you pass the **Ca'n Penasso** restaurant at the cut-off for the village of Bunyola. Continuing straight you will soon come to the grand country mansion of **Alfábia**. Beyond the baroque façade the entrance doorway is crowned with an important *mudéjar* ceiling dating from the 14th century. The house itself dates from the latter part of the 18th century, while the fabulous surrounding garden is the sum of a group of smaller gardens which reflect everything from the Arab *huerto* to the romantic gardens of 150 years ago.

Back in the car, you begin the climb to the **Coll de Sóller**. The road switches back and forth 28 times on the way up and 30 times on the way down the other side. On both slopes it passes the entrances to the controversial tunnel linking Palma to Sóller.

The town of **Sóller** is entered by way of the first cut-off to the right, signposted to the *Centre*. Within a few dozen metres you arrive at **Plaça Sant Francesc**, with its baroque convent of the same name. Continuing by carrer Isabel II and struggling past the oncoming traffic, you arrive at the **Plaça d'Espanya** which, because

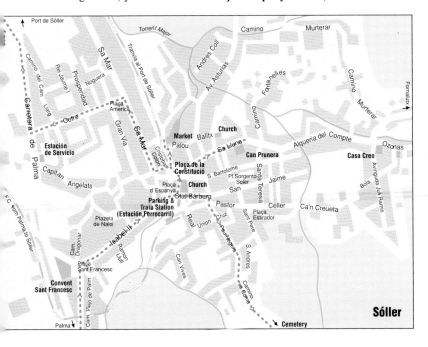

Sóller

Coastal hamlet of Llucalcari

of the taxi stand and the train station, seems to be in constant chaos. Find a place to park and walk along **Es Born** between the town hall and the parish church to reach the main square, **Plaça de la Constitució**. The façade of both the church and the Banco Hispano-Americano, next door, are two of the town's many examples of Modernist architecture. Walk down carrer Sa Lluna to get an idea of the town's narrow streets and then follow the tram tracks towards the market to look into the town's many small gardens.

For those interested in seeing more Modernist designs, a drive to the **town cemetery** is a must. From the square in front of the train station, enter carrer Santa Bárbara and turn right into the third street, carrer Sant Nicolau. Continue straight past a slight jog to the left and up carrer Pau Noguera, until the cemetery is distinguished by a stand of cypress trees.

To leave town in the direction of Deià and Valldemossa, leave the centre following the signs for the port along carrer Sa Mar and carrer Cetre. Once on the ring highway, turn right for a few hundred metres until you see the turn-off for Deià to the left. The highway climbs past the stately mansion of **Son Angelats** on the left. About 4km (2½ miles) further on you will pass over the highest point on the road. Drive between two old houses and find a cut-off to the right. At the intersection there is a sign for the restaurant **Bens D'Avall**. Even though there is a long, steep downhill drive to get to this restaurant, it is highly recommended.

Continuing on, you will pass the tiny coastal hamlet of **Lluc-Alcari** (at km 59) before the village of **Deià** appears. Once inside the urban area, park the car and walk up the winding carrer Puig, following the crosses which end at the parish church. Beside the hilltop **Església de Sant Joan Bautista** is the cemetery – the resting place of Mallorca's most famous adopted son. The small flat stone says simply: 'Robert Graves, Poet'. As might be expected, Graves acted as a magnet to many would-be painters and writers, and the village has amassed a small colony of artists of varying abilities.

Shortly after leaving Deià it is worth noting the olive groves and rocks as the road begins its climb towards the house/museum of **Son Marroig**. Once owned by the Archduke Luis Salvador, the house not only contains many souvenirs of his times in Mallorca, but is also the epitome of a seignorial mansion of centuries past. The garden boasts a small marble **temple**, the original of which dates from the time of the Archduke. From the temple there is a splendid view of the famous islet **Na Foradada**.

After passing various stately *possessions* (mansions), most of which were also owned by the Archduke at the turn of the century, you arrive at the top of a rise beside the **Can Costa** restaurant. Opposite is a narrow, climbing entranceway with a wall sign saying *Ermita*. It is the entrance to the hermitage of **Trinidat**, home to a small community of hermits. The doorway is often closed, but by ringing the bell and asking politely if you may visit the chapel, you will be admitted.

'Via Crusis' in Deiá

Turning left just past the petrol station, it is less than a minute's drive through a long line of sycamore trees to **Valldemossa**. At the curve in the road there is a large parking lot on the left. Leave your car and enter the village on foot by way of carrer Blanquerna. This village has been home to four VIP residents: Frédéric Chopin, George Sand, the Archduke Luis Salvador and Mallorca's only saint, Santa Catalina Thomás.

The obligatory sights in Valldemossa are the **Cartoixa** and the **Palau de Rei Sanç**, but if you don't spend an hour walking through the old town you have missed Valldemossa (see *Pick and Mix*, Route 5). The narrow stone streets around the **Plaça Sant Catalina Thomás**, their walls festooned with potted flowers, have inspired such inter-

Marble temple, Son Marroig garden

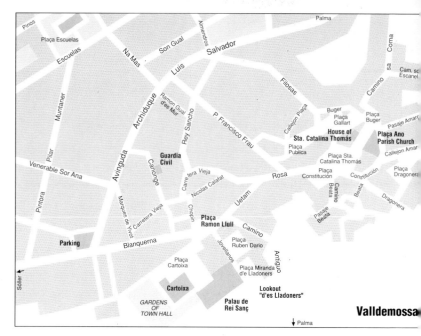

nationally respected artists as Nils Burwitz and Bruno Zupan, now both residents, and the beloved Mallorcan painter, Coll Bardolet. We suggest you stop for a coffee and a local speciality, *coca de patata*, in the **Plaça Ramon Llull** or, alternatively, a delicious *cocarois* in the **Cafeteria Romaní**, next to the car lot.

Leaving Valldemossa along the through road, the **Avinguda Archiduque Luis Salvador**, you will see above the road, directly ahead, an elegant *possessió* with a square tower. Recent investigation has revealed that this house, **Sa Coma**, was also owned by the Archduke, albeit for only a short time. From the first curve the road winds its way down the valley, passing other *possessions* such as **Son Salvat** and **Son Brondo**, before it reaches the flat on its way back to Palma.

The Cartoixa, Valldemossa

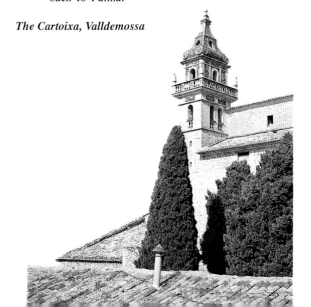

Day 3

Faro Formentor

Caves of Campanet; Roman bridge; lobster soup in Pollença; Roman ruins in Alcúdia; church museum.

The trip to the lighthouse on **Cap de Formentor** can be done in either one or two days. If you decide upon the two-day option we suggest you phone ahead to a hotel in the port of **Pollença** to book a room − the town is often fully booked. If you decide to go for two days you will have time to visit the towns of Santa Maria, Binissalem and Inca (see _Pick and Mix_, Route 3).

Six kilometres (3.7 miles) beyond Inca, pass **Campanet** and turn left at the _Coves de Campanet_ sign, 2½km (1½ miles) further along. Within a kilometre you are confronted by the 13th-century **Oratori de Sant Miquel**. Declared a national monument, it is a favourite place for weddings and is the site of great festivities at Easter. The **Coves de Campanet** are only a short kilometre from the small chapel. The interior of the caves is well presented, evidence that a lot of thinking went into the design stages − this is no underground circus.

Ses Coves de Campanet

Turn right after leaving the parking area onto a secondary highway which runs the length of the **Vall de Sant Miquel**. Between the comparatively green foothills to the left of the road appears the domed shape of **Tomir**. At slightly over 1,100m (3,608ft), it is Mallorca's third highest mountain after Puig Major and Massanella.

At the stop sign, turn left onto the PM-220. In the distance are the jagged peaks of the **Serra del Cavall Bernat**. Passing through the shadow of the hilltop hermitage of **Nostra Senyora del Puig**, follow the highway in its right-hand curve until you see a roundabout on the right. From the sail-like monument, which is dedicated to Pollensian poet Miquel Costa i Llobera, you can look into the town of Pollença, along the **Via Pollentia** towards the bell tower of the parish church. Looking to the left you can follow the steps leading to El Calvari. The 365-step climb to **El Calvari** is tiring, but a must. Although the oratory dates from the last century, it houses a statue of the Virgin some 600 years older.

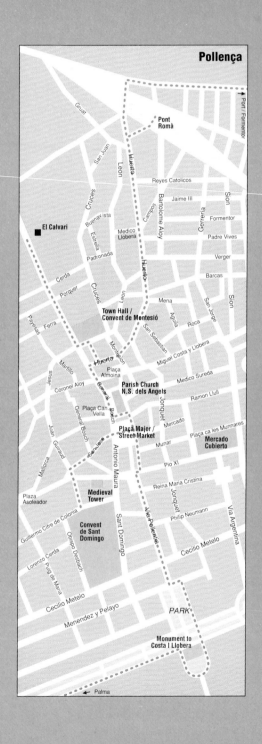

It is best to park the car nearby and walk. On Sunday the **Plaça Major** is a hive of activity, with the weekly market taking up any space not used by the outdoor cafés. In front, the 14th-century parish church, **Nostra Senyora dels Angels**, was built by the Knights Templar and later owned by the Knights of Sant Joan de Malta. The nearby **Convent de Sant Domingo**, with its outstanding cloister and museum, is home to art and music festivals, and also well worth a visit. Another interesting building, the **Convent de Montesió**, was built by the Jesuits in 1738 in the baroque style of the day. Next to it is the city hall, which was once a Jesuit college.

If you skirt the centre of town by car and reach the carrer Huerto, you can visit the **Pont Romà** as you leave for the port. Although the origins of the bridge are obscure, it is now thought to be part of the canal system built by the Romans in the 2nd century AD.

Continue on the same street and turn right towards the **Port de Pollença** at the next intersection. The scenery along highway PM-220 is being destroyed by housing developments and warehouses.

Getting to the heart of the port is simply a matter of not changing direction until you get to the water's edge. Once there, you have a choice of continuing out onto the pier or turning either left or right to a long strip of hotels. Some, such as Sis Pins and Illa d'Or, have maintained their original charm. If you have decided to stay for the night, a visit to the hotel reception will provide information about 'what's on' in the port, plus a guide to the many good restaurants. A local speciality is the *caldereta de llangosta*, which is served at **La Lonja** on the wharf.

Don't be fooled by the morning stillness of the bay. The habitual *gregal* – the northeast wind – has blessed the place as a windsurfers' paradise. Athletes such as Eduardo Bellini, many times Spanish and European champion, come from here.

The street called carretera de Formentor, one street behind the front-line carrer Anglada Camarasa, runs parallel to the curve of the waterfront in the direction of the **Formentor Peninsula**. The

Pollença bay

The 'lone pine of Formentor'

highway, the PM-221, makes a hard left turn at the airforce base and begins to climb quite quickly until it arrives at the **Mirador de la Creueta**. The view down to the small island of **El Colomer** is one of the best known on Mallorca. The road runs in and out of rocks and pine forest, switching from one side of the peninsula to the other, providing spectacular views of the **Badia de Pollença** and the Mediterranean. At the cut-off for the **Hotel Formentor**, turn left and continue towards **Cap de Formentor** (11km/7 miles).

On one flat stretch passing between low rock walls, you can see the old houses of **Cases Velles de Formentor**, which was where one of Pollença's most famous citizens, the poet Costa i Llobera, spent much of his life. Passing above **Cala Figuera**, to the left you can see in the distance a lone pine tree. For the Mallorcans it brings calls to mind one of the poet's most famous poems, *Es pi de Formentor*.

Statue of poet Costa i Llobera

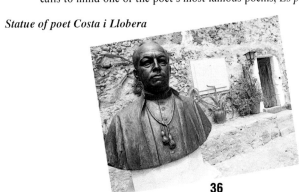

From the lighthouse at Cap de Formentor, the first headland which can be seen to the right (southeast) is **Cap des Pinar**, which divides the Badia de Pollença from the Badia d'Alcúdia. Beyond that is the peak of **Cap Ferrutx**, and further towards the horizon is the headland of **Cap des Freu**. On a good day you can see **Menorca** 25 nautical miles to the east.

Retired lighthouse-keeper, Rafael Alberti Martorell

In all likelihood you'll be back at your hotel in time for lunch, or at least a swim. Then it's back towards the port for the next stage of the journey.

The seaside highway passes the often-photographed panorama of the 'pines against the mountains', which has become the area's hallmark. Even though the buildings seem to stretch out to infinity, we are happy to report that there is still a bit of nature intact here – the **Albufereta swampland** – before the next town.

The skyline of **Alcúdia** is, like that of all of Mallorca's villages, dominated by its parish church. Closer inspection of the town reveals interesting sights to explore. The ruins of the 1st-century BC Roman village of **Pollentia** and the **Teatre Romà** are examples. The city walls alone justify a walk around, and the museum inside the parish church – the **Església de Sant Jaume** – is a must (see *Pick and Mix*, Route 10) before setting off for Palma again.

DAY 4

Andratx and Banyalbufa

Beverly Hills of Europe; Dragonera; lunch overlooking the terraces; tiny 'calas'.

Begin this route on Mallorca's number one highway, the PM-1. Bypassing the private Castell de Bendinat, Palma Nova, Magaluf, Costa d'en Blanes (Marineland) and Santa Ponça, it runs the gauntlet of the long line of discos, restaurants and souvenir shops of Peguera before arriving at the cut-off for Camp de Mar to the left.

Camp de Mar lies between **Cap des Llamp** to the right and **Cap Andritxol** to the left. The bay's most notable feature is the small islet in the middle, accessible by a wooden bridge. The PM-102 highway carries on towards **Port d'Andratx** through pine forests which from time to time open up, offering a view of the coast.

Despite attempts to alter it, Port d'Andratx still maintains some of the fishing village charm that derives, with the trawlers and the few remaining buildings, from the early years of the 20th century.

Notable examples are the parish church, **Nostra Senyora del Carme** and the elegant hotel, **Villa Italia**. The area represents the most expensive real estate in Mallorca. Outlying areas such as the **Mola** and the closer **Cala Marmassem** have become the 'Beverly Hills of Europe'. On the other side of the port, reached by crossing a picturesque inlet called the **Torrent de Saluet**, is the yacht club and the site of a temporarily crisis-stopped building boom.

The **Miramar** restaurant has been open forever, a good sign. **Rocamar** is *the* place of late, and **Tim's Bar** still seems to be a favourite watering hole for the boating crowd.

From here there are boat tours to the island of **Dragonera** many times a day. Leave the port by car along the highway to Andratx. In the distance you see the two peaks of the **Es Glop** mountain. To enter Andratx, turn left at the crossroads towards Estellencs.

Andratx has been almost forgotten because of the attention concentrated on Port d'Andratx. But the parent town collects the taxes and, no doubt, smiles all the way to the bank about the success of her port. Andratx began as a refuge for Christian settlers and was the home of both the Bishop of Barcelona and King Jaume I in the 13th century.

'Indiano' house in S'Arracó

When you arrive at the **Plaça del Pou**, follow the signs for S'Arracó and Sant Telm. On the outer edge of Andratx, the *possessió* of **Sa Font** still displays much of the splendour it enjoyed in its heyday as a producer of olive oil.

The tiny village of **S'Arracó** grew up around the **Chapel of Santo Cristo**. A turn-of-the-20th-century guide book tells of the 'cart journey [from here] to Palma lasting nine hours'. These days the village boasts what is, without doubt, the best collection of *indianos* (houses built by Mallorcans returning from the colonies) to be found anywhere on the island. Consequently, the village is an obligatory stop for students and lovers of architecture.

If getting to the end of the road is a must, then continue on to **Sant Telm**. Besides the **Castell de Sant Telm**, which was ordered to be built by King Jaume II as a hospital for sailors in the latter part of the 13th century, the only other 'attraction' is a view of the island of Dragonera with an ancient look-out tower *(atalaya)* 360m (1,181ft) above sea level.

Cala Estellencs

Returning to Andratx, you enter the town by turning left at a sign to Palma and right at the main road (**Joan Carles I**). Turn left again at the sign reading Estellencs 18km. From there the road climbs in front of the 'castle' of **Son Más**. History has it that in 1578, some 47 years after its construction, the tower was defended from a group of Arab pirates by the wet nurse of Captain Francesc Desmás.

The c-710 climbs past the cemetery and into the pine forest where, after passing the highest point, there is often a noticeable change in the climate. It is here that you will get your first breath of sea breeze. Soon, at km103, you'll be getting out your camera and, at km99 you'll see the first building since leaving Andratx — the bar/restaurant **Es Grau** and the **Mirador de Ricard Roca**. Because of the tour buses which habitually stop to refresh their passengers, we suggest you wait two or three kilometres more and stop for lunch at the **Coll des Pi** restaurant. Here you can look out over the terraced hillsides of Estellencs (Es-ta-yencs).

To reach **Cala Estellencs**, immediately upon entering the village turn sharply downward to the left onto carrer Eusebi Pascual, and follow it to the sea. The rocky inlet is ringed by tiny boathouses in which the fishermen keep their nets and gear. Up the hill in the village, the most interesting building is the ancient **Church of Sant Joan Bautista**, erected in 1422. But the look and layout of the town generally, which dates back to Arab times, makes it worth a walk around.

From the public wash house onward, the highway passes through

Sa Granja

an array of cultivated terraces on its way to one of the island's best known lookout points, the tower of the **Mirador de Ses Animes**.

Banyalbufar is considered the island's best example of felicitous land use. The terracing of the steep hillsides has been elevated to an art around the village. On the surrounding embankment the villagers once cultivated the now-legendary *malvasia* wine. Although the wine is no more, its name lives on in local parlance as a synonym for 'marvellous'. The **Hotel Mar i Vent** was once a summer retreat for many Palmanians during the 1940s. Its restaurant, which serves Mallorcan cuisine, still has a long list of fans.

The highway from Banyalbufar is newly asphalted and provides a well deserved rest for weary drivers. You pass a cut-off for the **Port des Canonge**, but as this is the most difficult road on Mallorca, it will have to wait for another day. At the next intersection keep right, in the direction of Esporles, and 1.5km (1mile) further on is the house/museum **Sa Granja** (see *Pick and Mix*, Route 9).

You'll then pass through Esporles along the side of the **Torrent de Sant Pere**. The textile mills which once supported the town have disappeared, and the village is once again living on the bounty of its citrus groves. After leaving the main street of Esporles, turn left at the petrol station and follow the signs to Palma.

DAY 5

Inca and Lluc

Leather in Inca; Leap of the Beautiful Lady; Lluc Monastery; hairpin bends near Puig Roig; 13th-century hermitage; Sa Calobra.

To get to Inca, use the PM-27 and the connecting highway C-713. Both begin in Palma by way of carrer Aragó (the complete route is described in *Pick and Mix*, Route 3). Enter **Inca** via the first cut-off to the left, just before the blue and white Ford warehouse. Once on **Avinguda General Luque**, you are confronted by a disgraceful display of signs, each trying to entice you to one or another leather factory. If the companies themselves aren't embarrassed, the city should be. With the arrival of 'European prices' bargains are few and far between and we can only advise you to shop around.

Since the city, replete with narrow one-way streets and difficult-to-find street signs, is complicated to negotiate, we suggest that you return to the main through highway (**Avinguda Rei Jaume I**) and re-enter the city further along, at the traffic-light intersection for Llubí and Muro on one side and Inca and Lluc on the other. You may make a quick tour of the town centre by turning left around the **Plaça de Mallorca**, veering right at the split and passing the right side of the parish church of **Santa María la Mayor**. Follow the one-way streets past the **Plaça d'Espanya** and the city hall until you are forced to turn left in front of the **Celler Can Ripoll**. This restaurant, as well as other *cellers,* such as **Celler Ca N'Amer**,

Selva against mountains

Cloister of the monastery of Lluc

on carrer Miquel Durán, are well known for their Mallorcan dishes of roast suckling pig and fried lamb. Turning left onto carrer Murta, the street leads back to the **Plaça d'Orient**, from where you follow the signs towards Lluc and Selva.

The highway to Lluc, the PM-213, provides a postcard view of the parish church of **Selva** against the mountains. The church, the steps to which begin in the **Plaça Major**, contains one or two examples of Gothic religious art.

Following the highway north, you will pass under an arched bridge which leads to the Selva cemetery. **Caimari** lays nestled in the foothills of the mountains. In late summer the villagers can be seen in the fields collecting almonds during the day, and sitting by the road's edge chatting with their neighbours well into the night.

The road begins its uphill climb even before leaving the village. It crawls along the right-hand side of the gorge called the **Comellar de sa Cometa Negra**, and you'll see here the island's most dramatic example of hillside terracing, dating from many centuries ago. After crossing the first pass, the gorge changes sides and you arrive at the **Salt de la Bella Dona**, where it is said a beautiful lady was thrown into the gorge by her husband. (When he arrived back at Lluc, she was waiting to greet him.)

Openings in the pine forest provide spectacular views of the **Torrent des Guix**, which skirts the right-hand side of the highway. After the petrol station, which serves excellent coffee and pastries, you have a choice of turning right to visit the **Monasteri de Nostra Senyora de Lluc** or going left towards the mountain highway to **Sa Calobra**.

· **Lluc** is the religious centre of Mallorca. It is the home of the island's *patrona*, Nostra Senyora de Lluc and, as such, is the annual destination of tens of thousands of pilgrims. But the monastery is interesting to visitors of every creed, both for its historic interest and for the architectural interventions of such famous artists as Antoni Gaudí (see *Pick and Mix*, Route 2).

After passing the **Escora** restaurant on the mountain highway towards Sóller (and Sa Calobra), you arrive at a small lookout point. More or less at eye level across the valley you can see the abandoned Guardia Civil barracks and the houses of **Cosconar**, which are built into the cliff face in front of **Puig Roig**. Beneath you to the right is the **Torrent de Lluc** and to the left, the **Torrent des Gorg Blau**. The two join at the **Entreforc** and together run towards the sea as the well known **Torrent de Pareis**.

Passing under the arches of the aqueduct, turn immediately to the right and follow the signs to **Sa Calobra** (13kms/8 miles). The PMV-2141 is, without doubt, one of the most spectacular roads on the island. In the distance to the right at the switchback curve you have a spectacular view of **Puig Roig**, and to the left a breathtaking panorama of the road ahead. At this point the highway begins its descent rather seriously. From time to time you can see the serpentine road basking in the sun like an enormous snake. Eventually, you will pass the small house of **Es Bosc** on a flat to the left of the road and, later, the house of **Can Pou** where the road divides.

At the junction you are greeted by a veritable Christmas tree of direction and welcome signs. Turn left and follow the signs to **Cala Tuent** until you reach a small chapel at the road's highest point. This **Ermita de Sant Llorenç** dates from the 13th century. Considering that this road wasn't indicated on maps made in the late 1950s, the place must have enjoyed almost total isolation for hundreds of years. The view cannot be described as anything else but staggering.

Returning to the cut-off, turn downhill towards **Sa Calobra**. At the bottom of the road, either park and walk or drive to the left as far as the cul-de-sac and its *chiringuito* (roadside bar).

A short walk takes you through two tunnels and ends at the **Torrent de Pareis**. Close to the end of the short flight of stairs which descends from the tunnel to the beach is a small stone stage on which a concert is held in the early summer of each year. The adventurous can hike inland a short way between the walls of the gorge. The less adventurous can go for a swim between the cliffs. This may be the only beach on Mallorca where there are as many people taking pictures as swimming. From the top of the Sa Calobra road, the journey back to Palma will take a little over an hour.

View of Morro de sa Vaca in Sa Calobra

PICK & MIX

1. Hermitages

Architectural jewel; ruined castle; hermits in Sant Salvador; lunch in Randa; chapel in a cave; Ramón Llull's grammar school; dinner at the house of the devil.

Since the day King Jaume I reconquered Mallorca in the name of the Christians, the most religious among the population have sought out special places at which to worship or meditate. Some have found their solitude in caves, others on the island's highest peaks. Apart from a notable exception in Cala Portals Vells, the caves have all been lost. But the hilltop hermitages have not only survived, many have prospered to the end of the 20th century as sanctuaries and monasteries and are worthwhile visiting.

One of the most interesting is an oratory which crowns a small peak not far from the village of Alqueria Blanca. To get there, leave Palma by the airport highway and follow the signs to Santanyí, through Llucmajor and Campos.

Follow the road straight into **Santanyí** until you are confronted with an ancient wall breached by a large doorway. To the left are signs pointing to **Alqueria Blanca**. Following the C-717 it is possible to see the hilltop sanctuary off to the left. Just before arriving at the town there is a poorly marked left turn indicating *Oratori de Consolació.*

The **Oratori de Nostra Senyora de la Consolació** is one of the best-kept examples of true Mallorcan architecture on the island. It dates from the 17th century. Today the building is cared for by the 52 families of the *Amics del Santuari*, who are responsible for opening the site every day of the year. The age of the oratory is attested to by a date of 1677 on the patio wall and another of 1646 on a wooden altarpiece inside.

Turning left onto the main highway, pass through **Alqueria Blanca** and follow the signs

Castell de Santueri, Felanitx

Santuari de Sant Salvador

toward **Calonge**. Once you enter the village, follow the signs first to S'Horta, then to Felanitx. When passing through these small villages, note the many handicrafts shops such as *Trastos* (Calonge) and *Art i Fang* (S'Alqueria Blanca), which are both worth a visit. After **Es Carritxó** you will arrive at an intersection with a stone cross. Continue towards Felanitx, and about 2km (1¼ miles) further down the road you will find a turn-off to the right, which leads to the castle.

The **Castell de Santueri** is one of only three 'rock castles' on Mallorca. It is, like the other two (Alaró and Pollença), a fortified hilltop. The ruins date from virtually every period of Mallorca's past, each element being used or discarded by each occupying power.

To reach the **Santuari de Sant Salvador**, you must pass through **Felanitx**, a town which has the reputation of producing the best brains in Mallorca. A long list of Mallorcan politicians, writers, architects and intellectuals are proud Felanitxers. The town is worth a look around. The parish church of **Sant Miquel**, for example, has one of the best baroque façades on the island. Leaving the town is tricky. The best escape plan is to follow the signs to Sant Salvador/Porto Colom.

Two kilometres (1¼ miles) after the last building, you will be greeted by two neat stone pillars on top of which are small crosses. The secondary PMV-4011 is criss-crossed by a *Via Crusis* – 12 crosses at which pilgrims can pray on their way to the top. Just before **Santuari de Sant Salvador** an enormous cross overlooks the valley. The sanctuary, which was built in the 17th and 18th centuries, was home for two hermits until 1992, when, because of their advancing ages, they were moved to Valldemossa.

Unfortunately, there is no way to get to the next stop without negotiating Felanitx's central **Plaça d'Espanya**. From there turn towards Porreres. Midway through **Porreres**, you will find a half-hidden sign indicating Montesió straight ahead (beside one for

Palma to the right). At the edge of the village there is another, and soon thereafter a third sign leads to another secondary road lined by a baroque *Via Crusis*.

The **Santuari de Montesió** itself is in the Gothic style and houses many reminders of its erstwhile incarnation as a grammar school between the 16th to the 19th centuries.

The route to the **Puig de Randa** is by way of the PM-503 in the direction of **Montuíri**. After passing the **Church of Santa Creu** and the municipal cemetery, you continue along a narrow road part bounded by stone walls. At the Palma-Manacor highway, turn left. After about 1km (½ mile) you will see a sign indicating **Randa** (6km/4 miles). If you are interested in stopping for a late lunch or perhaps an afternoon snack, the **Celler Bar Randa** is one possibility. For dinner we suggest you try the restaurant **Es Recó de Randa**, which specialises in roast suckling pig.

Once you are on the mountain road, it is difficult to get lost. The first of Randa's three oratories is the **Santuari de Nostra Senyora de Gràcia**. The present chapel is built into an enormous cave in the cliff face, with an unprecedented view of the plain to the east and the south. The interior is baroque and holds an interesting

46

collection of altarpieces and paintings. Less interesting, but in better condition, is the oratory of **Sant Honorat**, which is located slightly higher up the road.

Nostra Senyora de Cura is often referred to simply as **Cura**. The fortress-like structure is made up of a series of monastic cells (which can be rented), a church, a small garden and the **Museum and Gramática of Ramón Llull**. There is an open picnic area and a restaurant as well. The museum is dedicated to Ramón Llull, Mallorca's 13th-century religious philosopher and teacher. It houses a collection of etchings which adorn the founder's manuscripts and other reminders of the sanctuary's former use as a school.

After leaving Randa head north to Algaida, where there is a choice of three eating places – **Hostal d'Algaida** (next to the petrol station on the main highway), **Can Dimoni** ('House of the Devil') for a rustic but authentic Mallorcan meal (also on the main highway) and **Es Cuatre Vents** (next to Can Dimoni) – before tackling the 35-minute drive back to Palma.

2. Mountain Passage

Pilgrims' Square; Blauets choir; lunch in Escorca; Puig Major military base; over the coll.

Leave Palma on carrer Aragó. When you arrive at the traffic lights under a fly-over, turn left to climb onto the *cintura* (the beltline highway). The right-hand lane leads immediately onto the PM-27 motorway in the direction of Santa María and Inca. After by-passing Inca, continue straight along the C-713, past a glass factory with what appears to be a medieval airport control tower. A few kilometres further along, right in the middle of the fertile plain of **Sa Pobla**,

Pont Romà, in Pollença

Road into mountains near Pollença

you come to the round-about turn-off for Pollença/Port de Pollença.

At times the highway runs through pine-covered mountains, and at other times it overlooks the picturesque valley with the mountains of the **Serra de Sant Vicenç** in the background. On top of a steep hillside to the right is the hermitage of **Nostra Senyora del Puig** with the *possessió* of **Son Brull** at its base.

Pollença, with its Pont Romà and Calvari climb, is worth a long visit, but with almost the entire *cordillera* ahead of you it is better to leave it for another day (see *Day 3*). After skirting the town along the bypass, you arrive at the cut-off for the port. Turn left at the sign indicating Lluc 20km/Sóller 52km.

Although the **Serra de Tramuntana**, as the mountain range is called, begins at Cap Formentor, highway C-710 originates in Pollença. As you drive straight into the mountains, on the left is the tooth-shaped mountain, **Cuculla de Fartáritx,** and next to it the **Puig de Ca de Miner**. The third peak, **Puig Tomir**, is one of Mallorca's highest at slightly over 1,102m (3,615ft).

The road begins to snake around the steep, calcareous rocks and passes a pair of 'road closed for snow' signs standing as summer reminders that Mallorca isn't always sunny. As you approach Tomir, you pass the houses of **Mortitx** and **Femenia Vell** and their newer, 18th-century neighbour, **Femenia Nou**. After passing the recreational area of **Menut i Binifaldó** at km16, a petrol station sign alerts you to the upcoming entrance to the **Monasteri de Nostra Senyora de Lluc** (Yuke), less than a kilometre ahead.

Greeted by a sign saying *Benvinguts Siau* (Welcome!), the traveller passes through an enormous stone entranceway leading into the gardens of the **Plaça dels Peregrins** (Pilgrims' Square). One of the many buildings lining the square is the town hall of the 'villa' of Escorca, the only municipality in Mallorca which doesn't have an

urban nucleus. The convent, dedicated to the Virgin de Lluc, *patrona* of the island, is visited each year by thousands of the faithful as well as tourists. Constructed during the 13th century, it is the residence of the Congregation of the Sacred Heart, a hospice and a museum. It also contains the **Sa Fonda** restaurant, as well as a communal kitchen for pilgrims and hikers who want to prepare their own meals. The baroque façade of the church hides an interior renovated by the Modernist architects Gaudí, Rubió and Reynés, who were also involved

Statue of the Virgin in Lluc Museum

in the construction of the *rosario* which winds up the hill behind the monastery. Each day at noon the **Blauets choir** sings praises to the Virgin in the church.

After returning to the highway you will soon arrive at the turn-off for Palma/Inca and the petrol station. Follow the sign towards Sa Calobra and Sóller (22 and 32km/13.6 and 19.8 miles, respectively). From here, after one last view overlooking the monastery, you set out on a long scenic drive which roughly follows the left-hand side of the **Torrent de Lluc**. Not far past the popular **Restaurante Escorca** (recommended), you arrive at a lookout point where there's a good overview not only of the Torrent de Lluc, but also of **Puig Roig** and the **Entreforc**, where Mallorca's famous **Torrent de Pareis** begins.

The road begins a gentle descent. Ahead is **Puig Major**, the island's highest peak at 1,445m (4,740ft). The road runs along the **Torrent des Gorg Blau** until it eventually crosses a bridge and passes under an aqueduct. Leaving the long twisting road to Sa Calobra for another trip (see Day 5), you continue on the c-713. After passing through a tunnel you will find

Gorg Blau reservoir

Serra de Tramuntana

a pull-off area where you can view the **Embalse des Gorg Blau**, one of the two principal reservoirs in the Mallorcan water supply system. Behind the reservoir is the island's second highest mountain, **Massanella**, as well as **Tossals** and **L'Ofre**.

Soon thereafter comes the second link in the water chain, the **Embalse de Cúbert**, and the military base at the foot of Puig Major. A second tunnel marks the highest point along this route and a view of the **Valle de Sóller**. Descending, you will pass the **Mirador de Ses Barques**, from which one has a bird's-eye-view of the port of Sóller, before arriving at the cut-off to Fornalutx.

Fornalutx, with its steep stone streets and its centuries-old houses, is considered one of the best-kept villages in Mallorca. The parish church dates from 1639, and many of the houses still retain remnants of Moorish paintings under the eaves.

Leave the village by way of carrer de Sant Bartomeu and descend through the lemon groves towards Sóller in the distance. As the road curves left, it leads across a riverbed to an intersection where there is a large stone terminal cross and a modern house (Ca Sa Creu) which marks, more or less, the beginning of Sóller.

Because of its geographical isolation from the rest of Mallorca, Sóller is unusual among the island's towns. It is worth a long walk around and a trip to the port (see *Pick and Mix*, Route 6). All that's between Sóller and Palma are some 30km (18.6 miles) of winding road and a range of mountains, the **Serra d'Alfábia**.

After climbing 25 hairpin bends, you pass an elegant country house, at the back of which is the Font des Teix mineral water bottling plant. At the 30th bend you will reach the **Coll** (pass) **de Sóller**. The way down is easier – there are only 28 hairpin bends.

After the final turn is the elegant mansion of **Alfábia** and its neighbour, the restaurant **Ses Porxeres** (reservations required). Leaving the mountains of the **Serra de Tramuntana** in your rear view mirror, drive towards the silhouette of Palma in the distance.

50

3. Mallorca's Interior

Traditional cloth-making; baroque bell towers; wine tasting in Consell; bullring in stone quarry; train station art; traditional market; lunch in a 'celler'; Junípero Serra's birthplace.

Mallorca's interior offers some special treats to those who make the effort to go and find them. Carrer Aragó takes you out of Palma and, via a dogleg directed by signs to Inca, leads you onto the PM-27 motorway. At a flyover, 8km (5 miles) further on, follow the signs to **Santa Maria del Camí**. An hour's stop here is a must. At No. 77 on the main through road is the **Artesania Textil Bujosa**, a well-known manufacturer of traditional Mallorcan cloth. The cloth is known as *roba de llengues* (yengos) because of its multi-coloured, tongue-shaped designs. Not far away, with its enormous bell tower, is the 17th-century **Convent dels Mínims** and the house-museum of **Can Conrado**. Another highlight of Santa María is the beautiful arched façade of the town hall, located in the **Plaça d'Espanya**.

The parish church of Santa Maria, situated in the nearby **Plaça Caidos**, has a baroque bell tower sheathed in blue ceramic tiles, reminiscent of the one in Valldemossa. The church houses an interesting altarpiece dating from the same period.

The highway to the next village provides a good opportunity to view the table top mountains of Alaró. Like Santa Mariía, **Consell** (Con-sey) is known for its antique shops, as well as for its homemade bread and wines. **Can Ribas**, on carrer Montanya, is open for you to try the best products of their vineyards, bottled under the label of *Herederos de Ribas*.

The name of the next village, **Binissalem**, is of Arabic origin. Wine production was introduced by the Romans and the town has

Grape harvest in Consell

long been famous for its wines (visit **Bodega de José L. Ferrer**) and the cheap products of the recently closed local distilleries. Walking tours have been published (by the town hall, carrer Concepció), guiding the sightseer to such historic sights as **Can Gelabert** and **Can Garriga**, the 18th-century parish church and the old cemetery, once the site of the mosque.

Further along the main highway you find a mini-golf course, go-kart arena, waterpark, wax museum, restaurant and children's playground, the **Foro de Mallorca**.

The road traverses the island's central plain, which was once the richest agricultural region in Mallorca, and skirts Inca to the south (see Day 5). Two hundred metres (219yds) after the petrol station is a traffic light and a sign directing you to the right to **Muro**. Before arriving at the village you will first cross over, then under, then over again, the abandoned Sa Pobla-Inca railway line.

Shortly after entering Muro, you come to the **Plaça de José Antonio Primo de Rivera** and the former **Convent dels Mínims** (1560). Its 'Renaissance' cloister was once the stage for battles between bulls and bulldogs.

To find the 'museum' indicated on the nearby sign, continue on carrer Santa Ana, and turn right at **Plaça Sant Martí** for one block. The **Museu Etnológic de Muro** is in the house-cum-museum of **Can Alomar**. It contains a large collection of Mallorcan memo-

Nils Burwitz, the Mallorcan artist, in the S'Estació gallery, Sineu

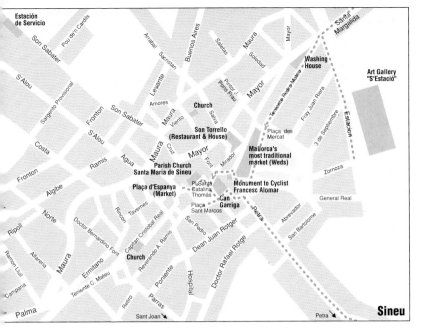

Sineu

rabilia. The area around the parish church, with its separate tower and bridge, is an excellent example of the integration of the modern with the historic. Last but not least in Muro comes the **Plaça de Toros**. This bullring holds up to 6,000 spectators and it is unique in that it is the only bullring rising from the very stone from which it was carved. In other words, this bullring was built *in* its own stone quarry.

To leave Muro in the direction of Sineu, follow the signs for Santa Margalida. Two hundred metres (219yds) after joining the PM-343 turn right at the crossroads towards Sineu (11km/6¾ miles). The PMV-3442 passes through bucolic countryside until it terminates near **Sineu**, the geographical centre of the island.

At the foot of a slight gradient, turn to the left towards the train station. The building has been restored as a rather unusual art gallery **S'Estació**, and is an excellent example of the recycling of old structures for modern use.

From the first road by which you entered the village, turn left, leaving the public washstand on your right, onto carrer Teniente Pedro Mateu, then follow it to the **Plaça des Mercat**. On Wednesday morning the braying of *burros* and the baaing of sheep is the background music for the locals at the island's most traditional market. Climb the hill to the right and turn left on carrer Església, which leads into **Plaça Santa Catalina Thomás** and **Plaça d'Espanya**, with its parish church of **Santa María de Sineu**.

One of the town's most spectacular historical buildings is **Can Garriga**, which fronts onto **Plaça Sant Marcos**, a short flight of stone steps down from the side of the parish church. Among other small palaces which lend Sineu a rustic charm is **Son Torelló (Toreó)**, now a restaurant situated on the street of the same name, and various *cellers* (say-airs) serving wine and food in traditional Mallorcan fashion, such as the **Celler Sa Font** in the Plaça d'Espanya.

53

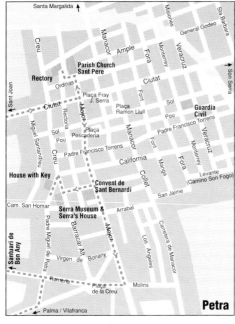

The road to **Petra**, the PM-330, is narrow as it runs along the valley towards Puig de sa Creu mountain. Enter Petra by way of the carrer de Ciutat. Three blocks on, you will encounter carrer Major. Turn left and continue one block until you come to the church of **Sant Pedro**. It was here that Petra's famous son, Fray Junípero Serra, was baptised on 24 November 1713. Serra established several missions in California that have grown into big cities, including San Francisco. Directly across the road from the church is the rectory with its small garden of ruined arches and statue of Valldemossan Catalina Thomás, Mallorca's only saint.

Return by way of carrer Major until you find on the right, one block past the intersection of carrer California, the **Convent de Sant Bernardí**, where the young Serra was educated. Carrer Junípero Serra, which runs beside the convent, leads to the house in which the missionary was born and to a museum. The humbleness of the tiny house led an American visitor to write in the guest book, 'It is amazing that someone who came from such humble beginnings began such a magnificent place as California.'

To leave town, continue along carrer Major until you reach carrer

Birthplace of Fray Junípero Serra

Molins. Turn right. At the Plaça de la Creu, continue along carrer Romeria, following the signs to the Santuari de Bon Any (the Sanctuary of the Good Year) built in 1600 by local people, grateful for a year of plentiful rains and bountiful harvests.

To get back to Palma after a long day in Mallorca's interior, return to Petra and, just before the Plaça de sa Creu, turn right and follow the road to **Vilafranca**. You may want to stop at one of the town's oft photographed shops on the main street, festooned with an enticing array of melons, aubergines, grapes and red peppers.

A half-day tour of Palma's museums, including a residence of 'walis' and kings; Bishop's Museum; La Roqueta ceramics; Spanish village; Gothic castle.

Even after a long historic tour of Palma (see Day 1) and a window-shopping spree in the commercial district, the city still has much more to offer.

Of the three principal museums, it is best to begin with the **Palau de l'Almudaina**, the Gothic palace of the Mallorcan kings, which dates back to before the Catalans arrived in the 13th century. The palace, which now serves as the official residence of King Juan Carlos when he is in Mallorca, retains architectural elements from the times of the Arab governors – the *walis* – when Palma was known as Medina Mayurka. The **Arab baths** and the **Arc de la**

Palau de l'Almudaina

Atarazana Real, which was used as an escape route by the last Arab governor at the time of the Christian conquest, are examples of these. Also of interest in the palace are the **Sala del Tinell** (Throne Room) and the **Capella de Santa Ana**, which was built in the 14th century.

Only a few metres away, along the carrer del Mirador, is the **Museu Diocesà** (Bishop's Museum). Worth a quick browse round, this contains mainly Mallorcan religious art dating from Roman times to the 19th century.

By following carrer Palau, carrer Pere Nolasco and carrer Portella, you will come to the most important of the island's museums – the **Museu de Mallorca**. As well as Gothic paintings and an inter-

Bellver Castle

esting collection of Islamic art, it has a section dedicated to a little known Mallorcan ceramic factory, **La Roqueta**, which is, in itself, worth the price of the ticket.

Another of Palma's main attractions is the **Pueblo Español** – over 100 replicas of Spain's most famous buildings brought together in one walled village. Such well-known buildings as the Alhambra of Granada and the Synagogue of Toledo rub elbows with the Puerta de Toledo and the Giralda Tower of Seville, interspersed with craft workshops and sidewalk cafés. The Pueblo is situated at carrer Poble Espanyol 39, not far from the Mallorcan Tennis Club.

The **Castell de Bellver**, located on a wooded hillside in the city suburb of El Terreno, is both tourist attraction in itself and a museum. Get to the castle by following the Avenguda Joan Miró and turning right onto carrer Camilo José Cela. It is a long winding road, which is best travelled by car. Erected in the 14th century, the castle is remarkably well preserved and is considered, along with the Cathedral and Sa Llotja, to be one of the jewels of Mallorcan architecture. The museum it contains (open every day except Sunday and holidays) documents episodes in Palma's long history. Built in a relatively short time, the building exhibits a great unity of Gothic style. However, in recent years there have been some avant-garde additions which have raised storms of protest.

From the castle it is an easy walk down through the forest by way of the steps in front of the main entranceway to have a light and leisurely *tapas* lunch at **Can Salvador** in **Plaça S'Aigua Dolça**.

5. Valldemossa

Visit to Valldemossa, home of Frederick Chopin, George Sand, Archduke Luis Salvador and Sant Catalina Thomás; lunch in an elegant country mansion.

Coming to Mallorca without visiting Valldemossa would be, to say the least, a great oversight. Getting there is straightforward. Leave Palma by way of carrer 31 de Desembre and follow the signs. The road is flat for much of its 18km (11 miles), beginning to climb only towards the end.

The beautiful skyline of **Valldemossa** is deservedly well known, dominated by the two bell towers of the parish church and the Cartoixa (for map of Valldemossa see page 32). The town, which is of Arab origin, is the highest inhabited centre in Mallorca. It has been the summer residence of a long list of VIPs for most of the past two centuries. The village was first 'internationalised' following the visit of Frederick Chopin and George Sand in the winter of 1838–9. Later it also became one of many residences of the Archduke Luis Salvador of Austria and of French artist J B Laurens.

Twentieth century residents have included the Nicaraguan poet, Rubén Darío, politician Antonio Maura, and a long list of internationally known artists, including Coll Bardolet, Nils Burwitz and Bruno Zupan. The village is also the birthplace of the young

Santa Catalina Thomás, Mallorca's only saint. Its famous residents have left it rich in both history and anecdote.

One of the oldest local monuments is the **Palau del Rei Sanç**, built in 1309 by King Jaume II of Mallorca and used by his son, Sanç. Ninety years later, King Martí of Aragón gave the palace to the Order of the Cartujos to found a monastery. At the beginning of the 18th century, the monks decided it was inadequate for their needs and began building the **Real Cartoixa de Jesús de Nazaret** next door.

Due to the extended duration of the construction, the impressive building, although basically baroque, exhibits neoclassical tendencies. The interior frescoes were painted in 1803 by Fray Manuel Bayeu, the brother-in-law of Goya.

The monks were forced to abandon the Cartoixa in 1835 under the disentailment laws and shortly thereafter the structure was divided and sold at public auction. Today the cells are owned by different families and are part of a museum dedicated to Chopin and the controversial Sand. The couple's short and quite disastrous stay, from 15 December 1838 to 12 February 1839, resulted in a series of compositions by the Polish composer and a book, *A Winter in Mallorca*, by Sand.

During the same century, the Palau del Rei Sanç was restored in the neo-Gothic style and furnished according to the times.

The village's other bell tower belongs to the 1245 parish church of **Sant Bartomeu**. Although the actual construction was begun in the 14th century, the façade wasn't finished until 500 years later. Beside the church on carrer Rectoria is a tiny chapel built where Santa Catalina was born in 1531. It was converted into an oratory in 1792. Every year, on 28 July, a young girl from the village is honoured as the *Beata* (the beatified one) in a procession.

Valldemossa at night

Surrounding Valldemossa are many stately *possessions*. Private mansions such as **Sa Coma**, **Son Gual** and **Son Moragues** have played important roles in the island's history. One, **Vista Mar**, 1½km (1 mile) along the road to Banyalbufar, is recommended for lunch or dinner.

Not far away, on the road to Deià, is the turn for the **Ermita de Trinidat**, a 17th-century hermitage which was the 'mother house' for hermits until 1921. Finally, stop at the village **bakery** on carrer Rosa to sample the local speciality, *coca de patata*, before setting off back down the hill for Palma.

6. Train from Palma to Sóller

Antique train trip; open tramvia to the port; lunch at Port de Sóller; modern church art.

One of the disadvantages of visiting Mallorca during the summer is the virtual impossibility of catching the 10.40am train to Sóller. But don't be discouraged; there are four others that are less crowded and which leave Palma at 8am, 1pm, 3.15pm and 7.45pm every day. The antique electric train leaves from a turn-of-the-century station in Palma's **Plaça d'Espanya** and stops en route in **Bunyola** before climbing over the mountains to **Sóller**.

The only difference between the tourist train and the others is that it stops for 10 minutes at the **Mirador del Pujol den Banya** to allow you a semi bird's-eye-view of Sóller. The train normally reaches Sóller in an hour, popping in and out of tunnels and clacking along through olive groves. On the downhill side of the journey you skirt the valley of Sóller, taking in panoramas different from any you'd see making the trip by car.

The journey ends at the Sóller train station on the **Plaça Espanya**. After checking the return train times at the ticket window (usually 6.45am, 9.15am, 11.50am, 2.10pm, 6.30pm) you can either walk the short block or two into the town centre or catch the *tramvia* to the port from its starting point in front of the station.

To reach the main square, the **Plaça Constitució**, turn right upon leaving the station and follow the tram tracks down the hill. The square is a good place to begin any tour of the town. A walk down **carrer Sa Lluna**, looking into open doorways, will illustrate that the social and architectural history of this village differs somewhat from that of the rest of the island. At No. 104 is one of Sóller's

Sóller train at Palma

Sóller train driver

best examples of Modernism, **Can Prunera**. Another walk, continuing along the tram tracks towards the market and turning off onto **carrer Romaguera**, then following it along the edge of the *torrent*, provides a different perspective (see Day 2). Still another walk is to leave the central square by way of carrer Bauza (sign to Port); some 30m (60ft) further along a jog right then a jog left puts you into carrer Cuadrado/carrer Capitan Angelats. After a few minutes you will arrive at a pair of large stone posts with the inscription 'Villa Palmera'. Through the gate is the **Jardi Botanic de Sóller** and the **Museu de Ciencies Naturales** in a turn-of-the-20th century manor. Much of the surrounding garden is used to display the flora of the Balearic islands. Nature lovers note that it is open every day except Mondays, more or less during shop business hours.

You can catch the *tramvia* to Port de Sóller (one leaves almost every half hour) either at the train station or at the corner of the main square and **carrer Cristobal Colón**. The open-air wagons pass behind some of the village houses, giving you a little closer look at the small gardens which adjoin virtually every house in Sóller. You pass through orange and lemon groves and then travel parallel to the main highway before entering the port.

The outskirts of Sóller

Port de Sóller

The tram stops every 100m (109yds) or so along the water's edge, so get off when you like. If you descend at the first stop, next to the **Plaça de la Torre**, you can hike around the beach, along the **Passeig de la Platja**, eventually arriving at the lighthouse. Continuing to the last stop, will bring you to the middle of the port. Beyond the train station is the public wharf, crowded with *golondrina* tour boats which cruise to such places as **Cala Tuent**, **Sa Calobra**, **Sa Foradada** and **Port Valldemossa**. Beyond are the white buildings of the naval station across the bay.

The hill above is the oldest part of the port, along with the *possessió* **Es Port**, which is now a hostel. Next to the hilltop church of **Santa Catalina** is a lookout point from which you have a view over the coast to the north. If you are seeking somewhere to eat, try either the **Restaurante Es Racó** or the **Celler d'es Port**, both on the way up the hill. Both serve typical Mallorcan food.

If you go to the tourist information office (carrer Almirante Abarzuza) you will have already found the parish church of **Sant Ramon de Penyafort**. Although quite new, and still under construction, it houses a fine pair of altarpieces.

For the return journey, because of the way the Sóller–Palma train hugs the mountainside, you should sit on the left side of the coach for the best view. If you find yourself on the right, don't fret – views improve about halfway up the mountain.

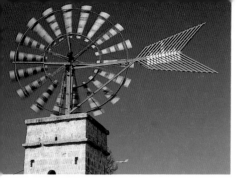

Windmill in Mallorcan national colours

Windmill country; Aquacity; Cap Blanc lighthouse; Talayotic village; Es Trenc; lunch on the fishermen's quay.

One of the images often associated with Mallorca is that of a windmill silhouetted against mountains. To get to the **Pla de Palma**, where the vast majority of the island's windmills are located, you should leave Palma by way of the **carrer Manacor**.

After passing the petrol station in the village of **Son Ferriol** you enter open farm country. The windmills are in various states of repair. Some are in total decay, others recently abandoned, while some have been restored and are turning in the wind. Many were refurbished during the 1973 fuel crisis and are now brightly painted, some in the colours of the local flag. An ironic historical note about the mills is that their original purpose was not to provide water for irrigation but rather to suck the marshland dry for farming.

Sa Casa Blanca, the next village, boasts one of the best known windmills on the island. On the right-hand side near the far edge of the urban area is a large 'geometric' mill which, because of its unusual neo-Arabic shape and accessible location, has been much photographed.

But to enter the heart of windmill country you must turn left when, after 1½km (0.9 miles), you arrive at a cut off flanked by two restaurants, **Es Control** and **Punta Son Gual**. The turn to the right puts you in the heart of the *pla*, the windmills finally set picturesquely against the mountains. On the left you pass the village of **Sant Jordi** on a hillock and, after crossing between two banks of runway lead-in lights, the road veers right to parallel the airport runway. At the stop sign, turn to continue on parallel to the runway and proceed to a roundabout-flyover-roundabout. Follow the signs to Santanyí. Continue on the PM-19 highway past exits Nos. 3 and 4, and

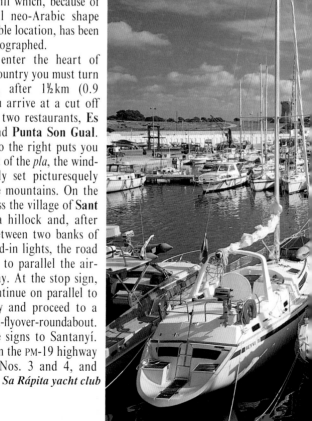

Sa Rápita yacht club

turn off at *salida* 5 in the direction of Cala Blava.

At the next roundabout you will be very near **Aquacity** (a worthwhile visit if you've brought the kids), with its towering water ramps and 'cardboard fortress' entrance. Until three years ago Mallorca did not have a single roundabout – today they've gone roundabout crazy. Go straight on to the next one! The PMV-6014 motorway has been newly surfaced to accommodate the dormitory villages which are springing up along the way. Unfortunately,

Talayotic village of Capocorb

many of the houses are excellent examples of the thesis that 'house buyers are victims of architects'.

When the **Cap Blanc** lighthouse finally comes into view at around km17, you are getting very close to the 150-m/492-ft-high cliff edge. Bear witness to the stunting effect of the strong winter wind upon the bushes. Since the **Far de Cap Blanc** is inhabited, there is

a 'Do not enter' sign on the gate in four languages. Skirting the compound to the right gives a good view back towards the Badia de Palma, while the route to the left provides a much better look at the lighthouse and the **Archipelago of Cabrera** on the horizon.

Continuing along the highway in front of the military encampment you drive into the harshest region of Mallorca. Until very recently, the land here was used for little else than grazing sheep and hunting. In total harmony with the uncharitable land, the Talayotic village of **Capocorb Vell** is found on a sharp right-hand curve. These ruins are not only historically important, they are also interesting for those who like to speculate about how life used to be 'in the good old days'.

Carrying on for another 7km (4.3 miles), you will come to a crossroad with an indication for S'Estanyol to the right along the PMV-6015. **S'Estanyol** and its neighbouring village, **Sa Ràpita**, are growing at a rapid pace as Mallorcans from the capital and other villages build summer homes. Because of the area's proximity to Mallorca's favourite waters for sailing, both centres have their own popular yacht clubs.

About 1km (½ mile) after the **La Rápita Yacht Club**, turn right at a sign indicating **Ses Covetes** and follow the secondary road to the village. As the entrance to Mallorca's most famous beach, **Es Trenc**, the village becomes a city-sized traffic jam every weekend. A few years ago, the village and the beach were almost unknown. The protest raised by an attempt to urbanise the area brought about the 'discovery' of the long strip of sand. But with or without the crowds, it is definitely a good place to take a dip.

Your last stop on the coast is **Colònia de Sant Jordi**, situated at the far end of the long white curve of Es Trenc beach. To get there by road, leave Ses Covetes and turn right at the first possible turn off, left at the next and then right at the main highway (PMV-6014), where you find signs reading Palma/Campos. Two kilometres (1⅓ miles) further on, turn southward towards Colòni de Sant Jordi.

Up until a few years ago *Sa Coloni* was a charming little seaside village. It has since turned into a sprawling metropolis. The restaurant **La Lonja**, on the fishermen's quay, is a good place for lunch and the beach to the left of the town beach is a good place for a swim.

Return to Palma by way of highway PM-604 to Campos and Llucmajor. If you go through Campos by way of the main street, stop at the **Pastelería Pomar** (on the right just past the parish church), which has the best pastries on the island.

Es Trenc beach

Villa Francisca, Bunyola

8. Serra de Tramuntana Foothills

Art Nouveau house; Valley of the Apples; lunch in a hermitage; climb to a castle; Gardens of Ayamans.

Probably the least known region of Mallorca is the area of the **Serra de Tramuntana** foothills.

To explore this fascinating region, leave Palma by way of carrer 31 de Desembre, which becomes highway C-711 past the city limits. Follow the signs towards Sóller, passing on the left the dormitory village of **Palmanyola**.

At km14, turn right towards **Bunyola** and follow the road upward till it crosses the Palma–Sóller railway tracks. At the stop sign, look directly to your left into the orchards where you will see, about ½km (a third of a mile) away, the tiled yellow spire of a house called **Villa Francisca**, which is one of the few intact examples of Modernism (Art Nouveau) on the island. The village itself has become better known lately for its serious overpopulation by cars than for its mountainside charm.

Exit the village by way of a left turn at the square onto carrer Major, climbing up through the village towards the mountains and highway PM-210, past stone walls and 500-year-old olive trees. On the left-hand side of the road is the majestic **Serra d'Alfábia**. After passing over the *coll* (pass) you see on the descent the fields of the

65

Vall d'Orient, with the arched balcony of **Son Perot** almost centred in the valley. Nearing **Orient**, a sign indicates the legendary *possessió* of **Comasema**, which lies in the heart of this 'Valley of the Apples', so called because of its many fruit orchards.

The village, the highest point of which stands at 455m (1,493ft), is easily dated to the 17th century. The house of **Cal Rei** dates from 1644 and, according to the local priest, Jaume Capó Villalonga, there has been a church in the village since the 14th century. The church's style is of the 16th and 17th centuries. The village is a popular spot for diners from other points on the island. If price is no consideration, **L'Hermitage**, located only 5 minutes drive out of Orient, is an ideal place for lunch, or try the suckling pig at the cheaper **Restaurant Orient** in town.

Continuing on in the direction of Alaró, you can see, to the left at km14, the *possessió* of **Sollerich**, which in its time was famous for its olives and olive oil. As the road continues its descent it runs between two table-top mountains. To the left of the road is the mountain of **S'Alcadena** and, to the right, the **Puig d'Alaró**, on top of which sits the rock castle of the same name. At km18, there is a cut off for the **Castell d'Alaró**.

On this side road you first pass the rustic mansion of **Son Curt** and then **Penyaflor**. After some 15 or 20 minutes of passable road you will arrive at **Es Pouet**, a rustic restaurant situated midway up the mountain.

There are two ways of getting up to Castell d'Alaró: climb from here or continue another 10 minutes in the car over a still worse road. Be forewarned: the second method will only postpone your hike. The castle is about the same distance from the end of the road as from Es Pouet.

Castell d'Alaró is one of Mallorca's three 'rock castles'. Chosen because of its obvious ease of fortification and its view of the surrounding countryside, this site has been used for defence and refuge since the first inhabitants arrived here more than 2,000 years ago.

Gardens in Can Ayamans

Alaró, like most of Mallorca's villages, is a maze of one-way streets and cul-de-sacs. The oldest part of town, around the central **Plaça de l'Ajuntament** (City Hall Square), may be worth a walk around. But be aware that it will look much like other towns along the route.

The exit from the village is via carrer Manyoles, in the direction of Inca and Lloseta. When you finally reach the crossroads, follow the signs to the left towards Lloseta (2km/1¼ miles).

Upon entering **Lloseta** (pronounced Yo-seta), continue into the centre and the **Plaça d'Espanya**. Next to the parish church is **Can Ayamans**, a large rose-coloured building in Historicist style, whose gardens are open to the public on Saturday and Sunday afternoons in summer. After your visit, continue along carrer Joan Carles I, which eventually takes you out of the village in the direction of Biniamar.

Biniamar is one of dozens of sleepy little towns in Mallorca which have been totally overlooked by the tourist industry. With

a bit of luck it will remain so. Apart from the interesting stone architecture around the **Plaça de sa Quintana**, the highlight of the village is a roofless church, the interior of which is now used as a football field. It is also novel to stop for a *café amb llet* (coffee with milk) in one of the bars, if only in order to compare the prices with those in Palma.

The PMV-2113 continues past groves and orchards of almond, olive, carob and fig trees, always with the mountain range on the left. As you turn left at the crossroads for the next village, the highway turns into the PMV-2112 and enters **Manoor de la Vall**. One of the focal points of this community is the 'typical' restaurant of **Turixant**. Another is the *possessió* of **Massanella**, which takes its name from Mallorca's second highest mountain.

Puig d'Alaró

Caimari, the next mountain village along the route, has two churches of interest. One is the church of the **Placeta Vella** with its Renaissance entranceway. The other is the parish church, situated on the edge of the **Plaça Major**.

Turning southward for the first time in the direction of Inca and Selva, you are treated to a spectacular view in your rear view mirror – Caimari nestled against the mountains. To explore **Selva** turn right in the town centre. A walk along carrer Angels to carrer Jaume Estelrich affords an overview of a vast portion of Mallorca. A street called **Aires de Muntanya** provides a finishing touch to this route as you drive back to Palma by way of Inca.

9. Galilea

Thirteenth-century monastery; mill town; Sa Granja; lunch in Galilea; Es Capdellà's lightning-struck church; 700 years of history on ceramic plaque.

To leave Palma in the direction of Establiments, ask for directions to Pryca via the carrer General Riera. After crossing over the *Viá de Cintura* (belt line) bridge, turn right for a visit to the 13th-century monastery at **Secar de la Real**. Within a few hundred metres you will find a sign indicating the monastery to the left. After parking either in front of, or beside, the church, enter the

spacious central cloister of the Cistercian monastery though a doorway under the porch roof on the left-hand side. The church was curiously renovated in Modernist style at the beginning of this century.

From here, return to the main road, turn right and proceed through **Establiments**, continuing straight on at the turn-off for Puigpunyent. After passing the seemingly interminable stone walls of the mansion of **Son Berga Nou**, you climb a slight gradient, passing the **Plaça del Rutló** on the left. After leaving the village, there is a series of interesting chalets along the highway and, at the road's highest point, a panorama of the **Vall de Esporles**. From here the highway snakes downward towards the village.

At the petrol station, the road joins the main road from Palma

Esporles – new town

Secar de la Real monastery

and enters **Esporles** through a long avenue of sycamore trees. The first part of Esporles, new town, or **Vilanova**, was built at the turn of this century when the village was heavily dependent upon the local textile industry. The oldest part of town is centred on the parish church, the **Església de Sant Pere Apóstol**, which is also on the main street near **Plaça d'Espanya**. On the other side of the **Torrent de Sant Pere** some of the streets still retain much of their original Mallorcan character.

A new highway leads 1½km (1mile) to the house/museum of **Sa Granja**. The site predates the Christian reconquest in 1229. First known as 'Alpic', it became a Cistercian monastery which was well known for its abundant water. The Italian style *loggia* and the gardens were both donated by the Fortuny family, who owned the house in the 18th century. The rest of the house maintains much of its Mallorcan layout, with the 'farm' chores being carried out on the lower floor, and the *planta noble* (noble floor) upstairs. The interior has been renovated as a museum of life in the 18th and 19th centuries in Mallorca complete with a picturesque medieval torture chamber.

Leave by way of the PMV-1101 (to Puigpunyent), through the **Vall de Superna**. The road passes through a typical Mallorcan forest of pine and holm oak (*encina*). Here you get your first look at 'the mountain which looks like a mountain', **Galatzó**, before descending to the village of **Puigpunyent**. For a good view of the area, try lunch at **Son Net**, a restaurant in a country manor outside the village.

69

Approaching Calviá

Continue through the village, following signs to Es Capdellà and the PMV-1032 highway. Once clear of the centre the road climbs quite steeply, turning back and forth on its way uphill. In less than 10 minutes, you will arrive in the tiny mountain village of **Galilea**. Although the village has recently been the site of too much uncontrolled building, the area around the tiny baroque church has kept its charm. In the **Plaça del Papa Pio XII** (next to the church) you can lunch with an excellent view as far as the sea. The restaurant, with outdoor tables and hanging picture menus (as always, looking positively unappetising), has some interesting Mallorcan desserts.

On the winding road down to **Es Capdellà** you are treated, from time to time, to views out over the **Costa de Calviá**. When you finally reach the plain, the castle-like *possessió* of **Son Claret** stands off to the right under the 'cone' of the mountain of Galatzó.

The only attraction in Es Capdellà seems to be the parish church. And, ironically, its drawing power is based purely upon the fact that it is completely out of place in the village. Its predecessor was struck by lightning. With luck, lightning will strike twice.

The terminal seat of the area is **Calviá**, 4km (2½ miles) away across fields of traditional farm vegetation – wheat, carob, olives and almonds. Approaching the village, a pharaonic sports complex is our introduction to the recent building boom, as is a similarly sized city hall (with **art gallery**) in the town centre. Calviá is rumoured to be the richest municipality in all of Spain.

Of historic interest is the Historicist style **Sant Joan Bautista** parish church, which was built in the last decade of the 19th century. A previous church, built between the 15th and 17th centuries, had fallen into such decay that the present church was built in its place. On the façade of the old city hall, which stands alongside the church, there is a large ceramic plaque depicting 700 years of the history of the village.

The easiest way to Palma is by the main highway. Return to the town centre and turn onto the Avinguda de Palma towards the coast. After 5km (3 miles) you will arrive at the overpass of the four-lane highway which will take you back to Palma.

If you're still game for a little more sightseeing, continue through Calviá along carrer Major till it rejoins the PMV-1034 towards Establiments. The road winds through a part of Mallorca which hasn't changed for hundreds of years. After km7, turn right onto a secondary road which first leads past the large farmhouse of **Valldurgent**, then climbs into the forested hillsides beyond. The *zona militar* signs are nothing to worry about, only a reminder to stay on the roadway. With spectacular views of the **Badia de Palma** (Palma Bay) and the **Castell de Bellver**, the road soon reaches the city's outskirts. Going straight over two roundabouts you will pass the social security hospital of **Son Dureta** and enter town via the carrer Andrea Doria.

10. Palma to Alcúdia

The next three routes have been planned as a three-day tour around the island of Mallorca. The first day covers: the walled city of Alcúdia; Pollentia; Roman theatre; lunch by the sea; Sanctuary of Sant Sebastiá; overnight in Cala Ratjada.

Leaving Palma on carrer Aragó and highway PM-27, you will arrive in Inca within 20 minutes, passing through Binissalem (see *Pick and Mix*, Route 3 for more details). The continuing highway, the C-713, enters the agricultural zone of Sa Pobla where endless expanses of market gardens line the road.

Approaching the walls of **Alcúdia** via the **Avinguda d'Inca**, leave the car around the **Es Clot** shopping centre. From here, walking along the town's walls to the right, you pass directly into the **Plaça Rector Ferragut** beside the parish church of **Sant Jaume**. Within the church – most of whose structure dates from 100 years ago – is the **Capella del Sant Cristo**, built in 1697, and a museum housing an interesting collection of religious relics and paintings dating back many centuries.

On the other side of the street is the **Museu Romà de Pollentia**, which holds a small collection of Roman finds from all over Mallorca. Also within the walls is the library **Can Toro** of the Bert Elsman Foundation (**carrer Serra**) and a museum in the **Centro Arqueológico Hispano-Americano** on carrer Ubellons. And don't forget the twice-weekly street market which overruns the **Avinguda de la Victória**, selling everything from watermelon slices to African folk art.

The walls themselves were first built in the 14th and 16th centuries. Those standing today escaped demolition when the parish church was erected in 1893. The two principal entrances of **Xara** and **Sant Sebastiá** have been recently restored.

Outside the walls lie the remains of one of the island's oldest archaeological sites – the Roman town of **Pollentia**. The ruins are

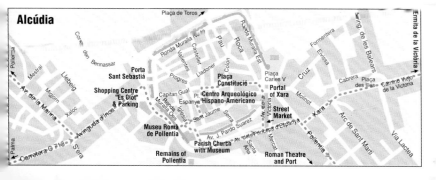

The walls of Alcúdia

only part of the settlement founded by the Roman consul Quinto Cecilio Metelo, after the conquest of Mallorca in 123BC.

To reach the **Teatre Romà**, follow the Avinguda dels Princeps d'Espanya to the traffic lights and turn right onto the road to the port. Within 500m (547yds) there is a sign to the right indicating the *Teatre Romà*. Follow the signs to the ruins, which date, like Pollentia, to the 2nd century BC.

Returning in the direction of Alcúdia, turn away from the town at the traffic lights and follow the signs towards Mal Pas on the way to the hermitage, the **Ermita de la Victòria**. The road winds along the rocky coastline, through developments and pine woods full of Sunday picnickers. Eventually it leads to the old church of the hermitage and the restaurant **Mirador,** where you should stop for lunch.

Es Port d'Alcúdia is 99 percent brand new. It consists of hundreds of souvenir shops, cafeterias, hotels, apartments and discotheques, plus a very well-kept beach. To the inland side of this development, sits the **Puig de Sant Martí**, Mallorca's number one hang-gliding peak. About 5km (3 miles) along the seaside highway you cross a low bridge and encounter, on the right, the entrance to the **Albufera**, a marshland preserve well known to ecologists all over Europe. At the end of the gravel road there is an orientation centre from which one can set out on various nature walks or watch a great variety of migratory water birds from well-appointed hides. With a bit of hiking you may also sight the herd of water buffalo imported to eat the canal weeds.

The ruins of Roman Pollentia, Alcúdia

Artá, viewed from the Santuari de Sant Salvador

The C-712, now in the county of Muro, passes through **Can Picafort** and later twists between the *possessió* of **Son Serra de Marina** and a small church, the **Oratorio de Sant Joan**. The road cuts though pine forests with a view of the fortress-like mountain of **Ferrutx,** its neighbour, **Morey**, and the high headland of **Sa Talaia Moreia**, before passing the cut off for **Colònia de Sant Pere**.

Far de Capdepera at Cala Ratjada

Enter **Artá** by carrer Sant Margalida, then turn onto carrer Monserrat Blanes, then carrer Antoni Blanes, and at the top of a gradient you will arrive at a 19th-century house with *poster* (stuck on) columns on a white façade. Turn left to pass **Plaça d'Espanya** and then, taking the first right on carrer Pou Nou, you will arrive at the town's highest point – the **Santuari de Sant Salvador**, the church which occupies the precinct of the ancient Arab *almudaina*. The village is spread out below, and you'll have good views of the parish church of the **Transfiguració del Senyor** and the broad plain to the north. The area is rich in archaeological remains, such as the megalithic village of **Ses Països**, which lies close to the abandoned train station on Avinguda Costa i Llobera.

73

An excellent side trip is along the road to the hermitage of **Betlem**, 10km (6¼ miles) to the north (leave town beside the climb to the sanctuary). It will take a minimum of one hour along the narrow highway, the PMV-3333. About halfway along the route you will see the fortified medieval tower of **Son Morei Vell**.

Highway C-715 is new all the way to its terminus at Cala Ratjada. Leave visiting Capdepera until the next part of this route, and continue to Mallorca's most easterly tip, the resort town of **Cala Ratjada**. We suggest you stay either at hotel **S'Entrador Playa** at the end of carrer Cala Aguya or at the in-town hotel **Ses Rotges** at carrer Rafael Blanes 21, with a Michelin-starred restaurant.

The evening is an excellent time for a walk to the **Far de Capdepera** (lighthouse) and a coffee in one of the bars along the **Muelle de Ribera** in the small fishing port, leaving a visit to the Gardens of Torre Cega until the morning.

11. The Northeast Coast

On the second day of our tour we visit Palace gardens; fortress of Capdepera; caves of Artá; lunch over Canyamel Bay; Lion Safari; Hams Caves; overnight in Porto Cristo.

The Cala Ratjada **Gardens of Torre Cega**, or 'The Green Mountain', as Camilo, the chief gardener, calls it, is the gardened hillside upon which sits **Can March**. The most important modern garden in Mallorca, it is home to a collection of contemporary sculptures by artists such as Auguste Rodin and Henry Moore. The grounds are open for viewing most days during the tourist season, but visits are by arrangment only. Tours are organised by the Tourist Office in the **Plaça dels Pins** (tel: 971 56 30 33). It is a visit worth planning.

Hill-top oratory and fortress in Capdepera

Much of the 2km (1¼ miles) road back to **Capdepera** is dominated by the view of the fortress on the hill top. Turning right onto the carrer de's Collegi, you eventually pass the **Plaça de l'Orient** on the left. If you want to climb to the castle here is a good place to leave the car. Turn right and climb up the stairs of the **Es Pla de'n Cosset**. To go by car, continue two more blocks to the carrer Major and turn right.

The medieval **Castell de Capdepera** was built

in the 14th century. Within its walls is the Gothic **Capella** (chapel) **de Nostra Senyora de la Esperança**, whose earliest mention dates back to the times of the Catalan conquest in the 13th century. It is situated on the spot where King Jaume I accepted the surrender of the Moors in 1231.

To leave the village, turn right on carrer Gómez Ulla and follow the signs for Son Servera. The PM-404 arrives after 3kms (1.9 miles) at a cut-off to the left for the Cuevas, which is quickly followed by another cut-off, with the right-hand option being Arta/Palma. Turn left (badly placed Cuevas de Artá sign over left shoulder) onto the PMV-4042, pass the strawberry-coloured golf club and follow the signs to the **Coves d'Artá**. You are permitted to take pictures during the half-hour long tour of these caves. The beach, the **Platja de Canyamel**, is reached by a footbridge from the parking lot on the left, leaving the built-up area near the cave entrance. The only way to get there is to walk. An alternative is to stop at the **Hostal Cuevas** and just look at it over lunch on the terrace.

To get to the **Torre de Canyamel**, you must return past the golf club and make two left turns, both with the fortress in full view. The medieval tower and museum are open to visitors. The key can be obtained in the restaurant. This is closed Sunday afternoon and all day Monday.

When you arrive back at the PM-404, turn towards Son Servera. If you are interested in a package holiday, you can turn left at the sign for 'Club de Golt/Costa de los Pinos' and head towards the seaside and the beach resorts of **Cala Bona**, **Cala Millor**, **Sa Coma** and **S'Illot**, which fuse into one another along the coast. If not, we suggest you continue straight in the direction of the town of Son Servera, from which you can bypass most of the area by following the signs towards Cala Millor until you see one for Porto Cristo.

The **Auto Safari** is situated on the right slightly after the turn-off for Sa Coma. It was moved to its present location from another not far away, where the animals were unhappy because of the encroaching urbanisation. Although the resident tapirs are from South America or Asia, the majority of residents are from Africa. In addition to rhinos, elephants, waterbucks and baboons, there is a mini-zoo for the children.

After the cut off for S'Illot, you will pass the tower of the summer discotheque Dhraa, perhaps the ugliest building in Mallorca.

Porto Cristo, which is the port of the town of Manacor, is best known as the home of the **Coves del Drac** and the **Coves dels Hams**. As the plan is to spend the night in the port, it is a good idea to visit one cave now and the other in the morning. For convenience we suggest the Coves del Hams. At the petrol station turn right onto the **Ronda del Oeste** and continue until the roundabout. Follow the signs toward Manacor and Palma. The caves, which are about 1km (½ mile) out of town on the left-hand side, were discovered by Pere Caldentey some 85 years ago. The subterranean lake is the site of a floating concert which coincides with the tours.

The area around the port is quite lively. After you have found a hotel (we suggest the **Castell del Hams** near the caves), it is worth taking a stroll down the slope of carrer Burdils, which parallels the beach, and down the steps to the fishermen's quay, following the edge of the inlet as it snakes into town. There are a few interesting architectural features to look at. One is in the square at the intersection of carrer del Mar and carrer Sant Jordi. Another is the church of **Nostra Senyora del Carme** in the square on carrer Çanglada.

12. The Southeast Coast

Ensaimadas in the Nautical Club; Drac Caves; Moorish tower; old fishing port of Colom; Ibizan-style city of Cala d'Or; a hilltop sanctuary.

The first stop on this third day of our route is for a breakfast of *ensaimadas* and coffee at the **Club Náutico**. Situated on the end of appropriately named carrer Vela, it provides a good view of the **Porto Cristo** across the inlet and the flotilla of pleasure yachts tied up below. Turn right at the end of the street onto Avinguda de Joan Servera Camps and left at the end; the next cut-off you will encounter will be at the **Coves del Drac**. This cave, like that of Hams, stages concerts on its underground lake.

Leaving the parking lot in front of the caves, the PMV-4014 highway heads southward towards Porto Colom. On the right-hand side of the road between the cut-offs for **Cala Romántica** and the **Calas de Mallorca** stands the ancient *possessió* of **Son Forteza Vell**. The central tower, which is completely separate from the surrounding house, dates back to Moorish times. Two kilometres (1.2 miles) after the turn-off for the **Cala Murada** you will arrive at a fork in the road. Turn left. You will soon encounter a petrol station, after which another left turn leads toward the port.

Porto Colom may be divided roughly into three parts: the old and new ports and the hotel zone. The first is reached by turning left by the old anchor as you enter, skirting the bay beside the **Passeig Miquel Massuti**. The area still retains some of the appeal it must have had at the beginning of the century when it served as

the export centre for local wines bound for France. Social activity revolves around the tiny church of **Sant Jaume**. The village's history is refelected in its street names, for example **Mar**, **Ancora** and **Velar** (Sea, Anchor and Sail), as well as the row of waterside boat sheds running alongside **Es Riuetó**.

The new port borders the right-hand side of the inlet and includes the yacht club, the fishing and customs wharf and the annual summer flotilla of boats which anchor in the shallow waters. The third section is reached by following the **Ronda del Creuer** around the shoreline of the **Ensenada de Sa Bassa Nova**. This is the main hotel area, wedged between the port and **Cala Marçal**.

Back at the crossroads of highway PMV-4012, turn south in the direction of Calonge/Cala d'Or. In **S'Horta**, the first village, follow the signs to Cala d'Or, even

Porto Colom

though they take you to the neighbouring village of **Calonge**. You will pass an antique shop called Trastos, which means 'junk', and the restaurant **Cas Senyor** before finding the last sign to **Cala d'Or** along PMV-4013.

Two things are attention grabbers about this popular tourist centre: it has grown from almost nothing to a major city in less than five years; and the architecture bears very little resemblance to that of the rest of Mallorca. In fact, the original promoter of the area, the Ibizan-born Pep Costa Ferrer, was so impressed with his native island that he imposed the Ibizan style upon the village which he established as 'Ses Puntetes' in 1933. Encompassing at least five inlets, one of which is Cala d'Or, the area has one of the best (and most expensive) yacht clubs in Mallorca.

The layout of Cala d'Or is extremely complex. To leave in the direction of the neighbouring town of Porto Petro, locate the end of Cala Llonga, in which the yacht club stands. Do not turn alongside the club. Two blocks further on you will find the Avinguda de sa Marina, where you will see a sign for Porto Petro at the first intersection.

With both centres growing at a furious pace, there are now hardly any fields left between the two villages. Although the small cafés on the upper esplanade by the port still maintain some of their original charm, **Porto Petro** is the site of enough superb examples of neo-gingerbread architecture to leave beholders speechless.

Porto Petro is the site of Mallorca's only **Club Med**. The well-known international club was founded as a campsite in Alcúdia some 40 years ago by the Belgian, Gérard Blitz.

From the tiny port there are two ways of getting to Santanyí. You can either carry on through the seaside village towards **Cala Mondragó**, or return to the main north/south highway through **S'Alqueria Blanca**. The second option affords a chance to visit one of the island's best kept hilltop sanctuaries, the **Oratori de Nostra Senyora**, situated on the outskirts of **Alqueria Blanca** (see *Pick and Mix*, Route 1), before arriving at the next village.

Santanyí has something which most other villages in Mallorca would like to have – Santanyí stone. This reddish stone, besides being the most attractive of all of Mallorca's sandstones, is also the most durable. Consequently, the village is in a much better state of repair than most of its neighbours. You will note that the houses have, as a distinguishing feature, a stone supporting the windowsill above the arched doorways. The local stone has been well known at least since the Middle Ages, when it was selected as the building material for such edifices as Sa Llotja in Palma and the Castellnovo in Naples.

A half-hour side trip to the picturesque **Cala Figuera** is a must before tackling the long trip back to the island's capital of Palma by way of Campos and Llucmajor.

Right, Cala Figuera

Nightlife

Life in Mallorca is as varied at night as it is at high noon. In the words of Santiago Rusiñol, the Mallorcans 'take the moon' as others 'take the sun'. Plays begin at 10pm. Cinemas have after-midnight *ciclos* which attract large crowds. Cafes are 'hopping' until way past midnight. And no one would dream of arriving at a restaurant for dinner before 9.30 or 10pm. In fact, Mallorcans are dedicated to almost any activity which keeps them from going home too early.

Cafés

Pub crawls, which may better be termed café crawls, are the most common activity. Mallorcan summer evenings are made for sitting on a terrace, sipping a beer or *café con hielo* and enjoying a *tertulia* (chat) until your eyelids are fighting to stay open. In Palma, the traditional cafés such as **Café Lírico** in **Plaça de la Reina** or **Bar Bosch,** not far away in **Plaça Joan Carles I** and **Café Sa Llotja**, at carrer Marina *2,* fill up around 10pm and stay full until their doors close at two or three in the morning.

But as Mallorca modernises, so does its nightlife. Today's *tertulias,* as often as not, take place in chic waterfront cafés in Porto Portals where, with a bit of luck, you may catch a glimpse of the Prince or Princess of Spain sitting at a nearby table. For *copas,* try **Capricho** and **DPP.** For late-night dining, try **Flanigans** or the very 'in'

Port de Pollença at night

pizzeria, **Diablito**. On warm evenings, head out to **Port Andratx** to see and be seen at **Tim's** or **Idó** or to dinner at **Rocamar**, **Miramar** or the **Club Naútico**. For those who fail to make it home before dawn breaks, the café and bakery **Consigna** is open from 7am for breakfast.

Discos

The narrow streets around Plaça Llotja in Palma have several late-night bars, while the more upmarket bars and discos are on the Avinguda Gabriel Roca near the Club de Mar marina. The **Club de Mar**, at the marina of the same name, is a smart disco popular with the yachting crowd and Palma's rich and famous. The long-established **Tito's Palace** on nearby Plaça Gomila has loud Europop and a laser light show. Along the Passeig Maritim, a younger crowd lines up for hours to get into the **Luna**, with inside and outside bars. *Discotecas* rarely start before 1am and entrance charges vary. Meanwhile, the 'slightly grey at the temples' set go dancing at the **Victoria Boite** (Passeig Maritim 32) or take *copas* at one of the many piano bars such as **Melody** (Passeig Maritim 3) or **Romance** (caller Marqués de la Cenia 87).

For a special treat, go the **Abaco** at carrer Sant Joan 1, with its heavenly atmosphere. If you like Abaco you may also like its big brother, **Abacanto**, a night club in an extravagantly renovated 19th-century country mansion a short way out of the city in the *barrio* of S'Indioteria. We suggest you go by taxi as it's hard to find.

In the other direction, in Magaluf, the discotheque **BCM** has set a new standard in evening entertainment for Mallorca. It often presents big name stars in its two levels. The upper level is for the soon-to-be-deaf crowd. The lower is for what the upstairs group calls *carozas* (carts). Anyone over 30 is a *caroza*. Interestingly, discos are not as popular as they were a few short years ago. A few 'mega-discos' have opened their doors and the smaller ones have fallen by the wayside.

Flamenco

For the best in flamenco go to **El Porton** at Passeig Maritim 32. If you're into *sevillanas* and *rocieros,* go to **El Patio de Triana** on carrer Joan Miró 15.

On Stage

The island hosts myriad other music possibilities, from classical guitar competitions and jazz festivals in Palma to piano recitals in Valldemossa and organ recitals in all of the main churches of the island. In summer, it seems that life on Mallorca becomes one long concert (see *Calendar of Special Events*).

Street theatre in Porto Petro

The **Auditorium**, at the Passeig Maritim 18, as well as music also stages theatre, opera, ballet and comedy. Check at the ticket office or tel: 971 23 47 35 for details. Palma's second theatre, the **Teatre Principal**, also stages events which are interesting from the visitor's point of view. Basically dedicated to theatre, it is also the venue for a wide variety of events from the International Billiard Tournament to film festivals of old movies in their original versions. It also hosts film series in such 'do-it-yourself' categories as mountain climbing, which don't need too much translation to be appreciated. The ticket office at Plaça Weyler 16, can fill you in on the details (tel: 971 72 55 48).

Dinner and Spectacle

A phenomenon which arrived with the tourists a few decades ago is the 'dinner and spectacle' evening. That they're still going strong is the best indication of their popularity. Places like **Es Fogueró** (not far from Palma airport) and its sister establishment **Es Fogueró Palace** (near Alcúdia) offer a dinner show of international and Spanish dancing. It is best to go with a group of friends so as not to get lost in the crowd, and book through a travel agent.

Other 'Spanish dancing' shows accompany dinner at the **Mallorca Royal Palace**, in Son Suñer and the **Paladium**, on the road to Cala Figuera (Calviá), where you can also spend a little money at the **Casino**. More skin and fewer frills are on offer at **Broadway,** Avinguda Joan Miró 118. Still more skin and absolutely no frills can be found at **Mustang Ranch**, in Palma.

For slightly more rustic evenings there are the *barbacoas*. Although there are many around the island, **Comte Mal-Son Termes** offers a feast and medieval joust combination which is, if nothing else, unique. Still more bizarre must be the Magaluf-based **Pirates' Adventure**. It all goes on while you're eating.

And maybe we shouldn't completely forget a night in. The majority of the middle to upper-class hotels are now fully wired with satellite TV, so you can watch a bit of 'back home' while resting up your day-weary feet for another big one tomorrow.

Right: detail from one of Palma's art galleries

For centuries, pork has been the cornerstone of the islanders' diet. In many cases it was the only meat they consumed during the course of the year. Consequently, the slaughtering of pigs has come down to the present day as an important cultural event on Mallorca. Every family, no matter how poor, fattened a pig a year and, after the *matança* (slaughter), filled the larder with sausages and chops. Also from the pig, they derived the lard which was the foundation of many dishes, both sweet and savoury.

It is the *sobrasada, butifarró, blanquet* and *camaiot* pork sausages which one sees hanging from the rafters of restaurants and delicatessens. All of them may be eaten either as they come or fried, which is how they are consumed during the popular *torrades* (cookouts) which normally go hand-in-hand with the religious *romerias* (mass pilgrimages) and the family barbecues by the roadside.

As throughout the entire Mediterranean, a rich variety of vegetables form the nucleus of many popular and economical recipes. Among them is the *sopes mallorquines,* perhaps the most popular of them all. Usually served hot, it is a winter dish (it may also be eaten cold) made up of *pa pagès* (peasant bread sliced extremely thin) and seasonal vegetables. An interesting variety is the *sopes de matances,* which includes small pieces of pork and *setas* (a type of mushroom).

Outdoor dining in Cala d'Or

eRIences

Also eaten in winter are *llom amb col,* a pork steak rolled in cabbage leaves and baked, and *arròs brut,* a soupy mixture of rice, meat and vegetables. Also very traditional, is *frit mallorquin.* Its mixture of fried potatoes, blood sausage, tripe and giblets, dripping in oil, is an aquired taste which can become a passion.

Elegant dining in the Anchorage Club, Illetes

In summer, vegetable dishes such as *trempó,* a salad of tomatoes, onion and green peppers, and *tumbet,* baked aubergines, potatoes and sweet red peppers covered in tomato sauce, are popular. *Aubergines farcides,* aubergines filled with minced meat and tomato sauce, is another favourite. Although there are as many fish dishes as there are varieties of fish, two dishes especially worth trying are *anfós al forn* (baked sea bass) and *caldereta de peix* (spiced fish stew or *bouillabaisse*). Also notable, but not strictly a Mallorcan dish, is *calamars farcits* (stuffed squid).

Savoury pastries, found in bakeries (*panadería*) or pastry shops (*pastelería*), make popular snacks. *Empanades* are small round pies filled with either meat or green peas; *coca de verdura* is similar to a pizza but is rectangular in shape and eaten cold. The *cocarois* is half-moon shaped and filled with *bledes,* a spinach-like green.

In the field of *dolç* (desserts) the variety is infinite, from the typical *gelat de ametla* served with *coca de gató* (almond ice cream with almond cake) to large star-shaped biscuits called *crespells* and *coques de patata* (a sweet bread speciality of Valldemossa). Also worth mentioning is *Greixonera de brossat,* a type of cheesecake. Of course, the queen of Mallorcan pasteries mustn't be overlooked. The *ensaimada,* a round spiral-shaped fluffy pastry, is made in a variety of sizes up to a half-metre in diameter.

85

Mirador restaurant, Alcúdia

Where to eat in Palma
Mallorcan

CA'N CARLOS
carrer de l'Aigua 5
Tel: 971 71 38 69
This lovely restaurant is one of the few serving authentic and delicious Mallorcan dishes.

CASA EDUARDO
Travessia Pesquera 4 (Mollet)
Tel: 971 72 11 82
Very popular, very busy fish restaurant located directly over the fish market. Reasonably priced dishes.

ES PARLAMENT
carrer Conquistador 11
Tel: 971 72 60 26 (paella de cego; closed Monday; no credit cards)
Located directly in the parliament building in a lovely setting. Good traditional food in this restaurant visited by politicians.

TABERNA DE LA BOVEDA
Passeig Sagrera 3
Tel: 971 71 48 63
Great *tapas* bar, full of life, known for the best *pa amb oli* (Mallorcan bread with garlic and tomato, cheese or ham) in Palma.

TABERNA DEL CARACOL
carrer San Alonso 2 (near the cathedral)
Tel: 971 71 49 08
Charming *tapas* bar with an open-plan kitchen serving some of the more unusual traditional dishes.

International

ASADOR TIERRA ARANDA
carrer de S'Aigo 5, off Avinguda Jaume III. Tel: 971 71 38 69
Meat, meat, meat... on the barbeque, in an old Palma mansion.

BAISAKHI
Passeig Maritim 8
Tel: 971 73 68 06
Excellent, elegant Indian restaurant – a change from Mediterranean food.

BON LLOC
carrer Sant Feliu 7
Tel: 971 71 86 17
Pleasant vegetarian restaurant with a set menu or *à la carte* dishes.

CASA GALLEGA
Passeig Maritim 25
Tel: 971 71 43 77
The Galicians excel at dishes using fresh seafood.

KOLDO ROYO
Passeig Maritim 3
Tel: 971 45 70 21
Cool dining room with dark mahogany furniture and white linen. Excellent Mediterranean/Basque cuisine with one Michelin star.

MEDITERRANEO 1930
Passeig Maritim 33
Tel: 971 45 88 77
A truly classic restaurant, where *tout Mallorca* gathers.

PORTO PI
Avinguda Joan Miró 174
Tel: 971 40 00 87
Good food in a lovely Mallorcan manor just outside Palma.

SHOGUN
carrer Camilo José Cela 14
Tel: 971 73 57 48 (closed Monday)
First-rate Japanese food. Elegant surroundings.

Where to eat Elsewhere
Mallorcan

When the Mallorcans dine out, they like to head for Algaida. Follow their example, and visit one the following three restaurants.

CAL DIMONI (Algaida)
Palma–Manacor road km21
Tel: 971 66 50 35
Sobrasadas (savoury sausages) hang from the ceiling waiting to be roasted over an open fire. Rustic, with reasonable prices.

ES 4 VENTS (Algaida)
Palma–Manacor road km21
Tel: 971 66 51 73
Closed Thursday.
Popular venue for large family Sunday lunches.

HOSTAL DI ALGAIDA (Algaida)
Palma–Manacor road km21
Tel: 971 66 51 09
Rustic coaching inn with delicious Mallorcan food.

SES PORXERES (Bunyola)
Sóller road km17
Tel: 971 61 31 10
Catalan cuisine. Game specialities recommended. Reservations required.

CAN QUET (Deià)
carrer Es Molí, s/n
Tel: 972 63 91 96
Mallorcan food served on a terrace with views of the mountains.

CELLER CA'N AMER (Inca)
carrer Pau 39
Tel: 971 50 12 61
Represented the Balearan cuisine at Expo 92 in Seville.

CELLER CAN RIPOL (Inca)
carrer Jaume Armengol 4
Tel: 971 50 00 24
A real Mallorcan *celler*. Slightly refined local cuisine, reasonable prices.

CA'N COSTA (Valldemossa)
Valldemossa–Deiá road, km2.5
Tel: 971 61 22 63 (Closed Tuesday)
Cosy and rustic.

LA LONJA (Port de Pollença)
Dique Moll
Tel: 971 53 00 23
Panoramic view. Excellent lobster stew.

MIRAMAR (Port d'Andratx)
carrer Mateo Bosch 22
Tel: 971 67 30 09
Fashionable dining at the water's edge.

FLANAGANS (Puerto Portals)
Harbour front
Tel: 971 67 61 17
Trendy waterside bar/restaurant with excellent *tapas* and special fish *paella*.

International

BEC-FI (Port de Pollença)
Avinguda Anglada Camarasa 91
Tel: 971 53 10 40
A large menu, plus leafy patio. Open summer only.

SON NET
Carretera Palma–Puigpunyent, km14
Tel: 971 61 40 57
Refined international cuisine and slick service in an old mill, or in summer beneath a massive tree on the terrace.

Ensaimadas, sweet Mallorcan pastries

Shopping

What To Buy

No one can say that Mallorca lacks a long tradition of commercial activity. Since ancient times it has been a centre of Mediterranean trade and has fostered a range of artistic and industrial activities which have created a substantial reputation for the island, both at home and abroad.

Until quite recently, some of the local *artesania*, such as ceramics and textiles, have occupied an important place in the local economy. But with the advent of better transport and communications with mainland production centres, and the diversion of the majority of qualified craftsmen to the tourist industry, the once common activities have been reduced almost entirely to serving the tourist market.

Glassmaking

Glassmaking, for example, is now done for the benefit of tourists only. Factories dating from the 1950s have been moved to tourist route locations and are open to both bus tours and casual passers-by. There are two glass-blowing factories which can be visited: **Lafiore**, at km11 on the road to Valldemossa, and **Gordiola**, which is just before Algaida on the Palma–Manacor highway. The latter glassworks also has two shops in **Palma** – one on carrer Jaume III and another at carrer Victória 2.

Pottery and Ceramics

Local pottery in Sineu market

Although many towns in Mallorca have a tradition of pottery and ceramic making, it is the tiny village of **Portol**, in the terminal of **Marratxí,** which has the most working kilns. As well as the childish red, white and green clay-figure whistles called *siurells,* which are said to have originated in Arab times, you will find examples of popular ceramic utensils made of reddish glazed clay.

In Palma, two good places to shop for ceramics, both traditional and artistic, are **Fet a má** at carrer Sant Miquel 52, and **L'Ocell de Foc,** located at carrer Pere Nolasc 8.

Jewellery shop

Cloth

Mallorcan cloth also has a good reputation. Until the beginning of the 20th century there were literally dozens of mills, both in Palma and in villages such as Sóller, Esporles, Santa Maria and Pollença. Their most popular product is the cloth known as **roba de llengües** ('cloth of tongues'), named for the colourful tongue-shaped patterns that are stamped on the woven cotton. It continues to be made in both Santa Maria and Pollença as well as in the capital city. One of the most traditional shops in the trade is **Herederos de Vicente Ribas** at carrer Sant Nicolau 10, in Palma, two shops up the hill from the church, on the left-hand side.

Bordados (crochet) is another speciality of Mallorcan traditional crafts. Today the machine has replaced the hand and it is only possible to find handmade examples of Mallorcan *bordados* in a few *pueblos* (Pollença, for example) and in Palma. **Casa Bonet** at Plaça Frederic Chopin 2, in Palma, is renowned for the work. In any shop, make sure you look for the label *Hecho a mano* or *Fet a má* to ensure items are handmade.

Woodcarving

The decline in Mallorca's olive oil industry has given rise to the use of olive wood for decorative purposes. **La Casa del Olivo**, at carrer Pescatería Vella 4, sells beautiful olive wood salad bowls.

Leather

The leather goods and shoe industry is, without doubt, one of the most important industrial activities on the island. With a

Bordados (crochet work)

Decorated for Christmas

craftsmen's tradition behind it, the industry began more than a century ago. But it was in the 1960s and '70s that it became known the world over. Inca is the home of most of the better-known brands and, as well as factory outlets, you can visit the factories themselves (see Day 5). When buying from the factory you can expect a small discount, but the days of bargains in Mallorca are now history. In Palma there are various shops which sell both rustic and high fashion leather goods and innumerable shoe stores carrying the entire range of Mallorcan-made shoes. For those looking for more elegant and modern footwear, there are several places in Palma: **Windsor**, at carrer Colón 3; **Passy**, **Camper** and **Charles Jourdan**, all on Avinguda Jaume III. For fashion leather goods, **Armando Dengra**, at carrer Palau Reial 19, is your best bet.

Making artificial pearls

Artificial Pearls

Since the beginning of the century, when the fabrication of artificial pearls began in Mallorca, Manacor has maintained a long lead in the industry. As well as **Orquidea** and **Majorica**, there are various smaller companies which compete for the tourist market. Although the tour to Manacor includes a 5-minute run-through of the manufacturing process, we strongly suggest you save the trip and buy the pearls from one of the outlets in Palma. The prices are very similar, you are treated better due to the lack of crowds and you don't waste a morning in Manacor. One official outlet of Orquidea is in the centre of the city at Plaça Joan Carles I 1. One Majorica outlet is at Avinguda Jaume III 11.

Wine and Liqueurs

Vineyards are found on two parts of the island: the area of Binissalem–Consell–Santa Maria, and the county of Felanitx. Among many, we recommend the *tintos* (red), **José L Ferrer**, **Franja Roja** of Binissalem and **Jaume Mesquida** of Porreres, and both the excellent reds and whites of **Herederos de Ribas** from Consell.

In the past, the local liqueurs were also notable. Today those producers who have persevered and who have gained the most acceptance are **Palo** and **Hierbas**, both of which are taken at the meal's end as a *digestivo*. In Palma, **Llofriu** specialises in Mallorcan spirits at carrer Sant Nicolau 22.

Sweets

A rich and varied Mallorcan speciality are the *dulces* or sweets. The variety which may be found at the local confectioner's is extensive but, without doubt, there is one which has gained in popularity above all others – the *ensaimada*. It is a soft, fluffy pastry made from wheat flour, lard and water. Circular in shape, it takes its form from an expanding spiral of snake-shaped rolled dough. It is sold plain or

Mallorcan sweets

filled with cream, whipped cream or the traditional pumpkin marmalade and, depending upon the season, topped with pieces of fruit or salty *sobrasada* sausage. They are sold in almost every bakery in the island, packaged in appropriately large, round boxes for 'export' (you will see scores of them in the departure lounge at the airport when you leave). **Forn Fondo** at carrer Unió 15 and **Forn des Teatre** at Plaça Weyle 9, are good places to buy in Palma. When in Campos, I recommend that you try the island's best pastry shop **Pomar**, at Plaça 20.

Antiques

Until the 1980s, buying antique pieces was simple and economical, for old furniture was being discarded in favour of formica tables and Naugahyde sofas and chairs. But demand for antiques has grown considerably in the past few years. So have the prices. Now the sale of everything antique, from small rustic wall cupboards once used

Shopping on Avinguda Jaume III

to hold the kitchen collection of wooden spoons, to pieces for enormous country houses, has boomed.

There are various well-known antique shops throughout the island, most notably in Santa Mariá, Consell, S'Alquería Blanca and Pollença. In Palma, **Antigüedades Delmonte**, La Rambla 8A, **Linares**, Plaça Almoina 4, and **Midge Dalton** at Plaça Mercat 20, are representative. Many interior design shops carry a large selection of period funishings and antiques. The most established are **Casa Juncosa**, carrer Sant Nicolau 12, and **Interior**, at carrer Sant Martí 6. Try the Rastro or flea market which takes over the Avinguda Gabriel Alomari Villalonga every Saturday morning.

Art

In the last 15 years there has been a veritable artistic renaissance on Mallorca. Although it is still too early to interpret the causes, no doubt it is connected to the general liberalisation which has influenced Mallorcan society since the coming of democracy, as well as the increased buying power of the residents. With the market potential of the rest of Europe close at hand, a growing number of foreign artists-in-residence and the growing visibility of a few Mallorcan artists, art galleries and cultural centres have proliferated in every part of the island. Pollença and Alcúdia both have galleries which exhibit local and foreign work. The gallery **S'Estació**, housed in the abandoned railway station of Sineu, specialises in the work of contemporary artists. Palma has many galleries and, because of the city's small size, they can all be reached without too much difficulty. Some of the most notable venues are the **Galería Altair,** at carrer Sant Jaume 15A, **Centro Pelaires**, on carrer Veri 3, **Ferrán Cano**, carrer de la Pau 3, **Quatre Gats**, carrer Sant Sebastiá 3, **Joaquin Mir**, carrer Concepció 38 and **Joan Oliver**, carrer Sant Marti 2.

Old shop in Palma's centre

Palma also boasts various 'cultural centres', most of which hold exhibitions on a regular basis: the City Hall's **Can Sollerich**, carrer Sant Cayetano 10, the **Govern Balear's Sa Llotja**, Passeig de Sagrera, that of the savings bank '**Sa Nostra**' in a newly renovated 18th-century building at carrer Concepció 12 and the **Círculo de Bellas Artes** at carrer Unió 5.

Other cultural centres in Palma are those of **Banca March** at carrer Sant Miquel 11, the **Caixa de Barcelona,** which is housed in a magnificently restored art nouveau building (formerly the Gran Hotel) on Plaça Weyler, carrer Unió, opened in 1992, and the **Centre Cultural de la Misericordia**, at Via Roma 1.

Shopping in Palma

For the shopper, the relatively small size of Palma is of great advantage. **Avinguda Jaume** III, as well as being the best-known street in the city, is also the newest. Although it is hard to believe, only 30 years ago the street didn't exist. Today it is one of Palma's most elegant avenues, lined with sophisticated shops offering men's and women's fashions as well as jewellery and gifts. **El Corte Inglès**, one of Spain's most popular department store chains, is represented at No. 15. For a thorough shopping spree don't forget the side streets of **Bonaire, Sta. Maria del Sepulcro, Sant Martí**, etc.

Following the broad street down its gentle slope, you'll find it branches at the **Plaça Joan Carles** I, in which is found the department store **C&A**. Turning onto the pedestrian street, the Passeig del Born, we find a small but interesting variety of shops ranging from the fashion accessories of **Loewe** and elegant high-street fashion for men, women and children at **Zara**, to the *alpargatas* (traditional rope shoes) of **Cesteria del Centro** at No. 18.

Returning to the square in front of C&A, turn right onto **carrer Unió**. On the left, at No. 5, is Palma's best known toy shop, **Arlequín**, which always has a wonderful window display that will send a shot of nostalgia through the veins of even the most jaded visitor. In **Plaça Sta. Catalina Thomás** you will find two chocolate shops, **Can Frasquet** and **Cas Net**, whose mouth-watering displays are difficult to resist.

After this, carrer Unió takes a dog-leg to the left and enters the pedestrian street **La Rambla**, which is the street of the flower sellers in Palma.

Returning to the Plaça Joan Carles I again, take **carrer Jovelanos** (near MacDonalds) to **carrer Pelaries,** on which you will find **Ereso**, one of the best bookshops in the city. Passing in front of the doorway of the shop, you enter **carrer Sant Nicolau**, named after the church nearby. This street, along with the areas around **Plaça Chopin** and **carrer Tous i Maroto**, is part of one of the busiest commercial districts of the city. Nearby are the chic boutiques of **carrer Verí**. The street is worth a stroll for its architecture, even if you are not interested in high fashion.

Continuing on Sant Nicolau, before climbing the stairs of **Pas d'en Quint** you will find the jeweller **Paradis** at No. 7. At the top of the stairs a turn to the left onto **carrer Jaume II** will take you past a **Gordiola** glass shop at No 14, and at No. 29 the well known **La Montaña** delicatessen, before continuing on to the Plaça Major. Alternatively, at the top of the stairs, enter the City Hall square (**Plaça de Cort**) and take the next left onto **carrer Colón**. There are a great variety of shops in this zone, some of which date back 100 years and have maintained the old store fronts. Examples are the knife shop on the corner of Plaça de Cort and a music shop, the **Antigua Casa Banqué**, at No. 56.

The main interest of Plaça Major is the outdoor craft market, which is held there Monday, Friday and Saturday mornings. From the enclosed square, under which is a touristy shopping mall, you may leave either by proceeding straight ahead onto **carrer Sant Miquel** or taking the right-hand exit and joining **carrer Sindicat**, where the shoe shops seem to go on forever and, traditionally, people used to go to find the cheapest prices.

On Sant Miquel you will pass a wide variety of clothing, hardware and pastry shops. One interesting shop, at No. 6, is the *alpargateria* **Fornés**, which sells all sorts of articles made of woven straw, from shoes to shopping bags. The street leads to **carrer des Oms (Olmos)**. The descent on the newly converted pedestrian street is between book and poster shops, opticians and the city's most popular photocopy stores, where, at times, there are queues for one and all. The bottom of the street again joins onto the Rambla after a few short minutes' walk.

Right, street market,
Alcudia

Calendar of Special Events

Art/Music and Local Village Festivals

Mallorca has become, in the course of the past few years, a cultural centre *par excellence*. As well as the village festivals, many of which are genuinely worth seeing, there are prestigious musical events that attract some of the world's finest musicians.

Four times a year, the tourist office publishes a booklet in English detailing all the major events scheduled for the following three months. Ask for *Events* at the Tourist Office.

The local village festivals began as religious celebrations dedicated to the patron saint of each village. Although they continue to have significance for many, to the outsider they often appear to have degenerated to nothing more than a rock band *verbena* (street dance) and a street market.

But the traditions have not been completely lost. The **cossiers**, celebrated in Algaida and Montuíri, are particularly worth attending. This celebration is first mentioned in 15th-century documents as the *ball de Cosi*, leading to speculation that its origins were Scottish. Originally, the dance was performed by seven men, one of whom acted the part of a *dama*. Dressed in colourful ribboned costumes with bells and straw hats, they dance through the village streets to the accompaniment of local musicians. In a ritualised fight of good over evil, the *demoni* carries a big stick with which he threatens both the dancers and the public. In the end, the devil is vanquished and falls at the feet of the *dama*. Today, the female character is played by a woman.

The **cavallets** of Felanitx have a religious thrust. Children carrying *papier-mâché* horses and dressed in

'Cossier' dancer

costumes gallop around town to the tune of the *xeremia* (bagpipe), *fabiol* (small flute) and *tamborí* (small drum). They begin their dancing in church and are followed through the streets by *cabezudos* (big heads) and the traditional *gigants* (giants).

A Spanish celebration which attracts equally large crowds in Mallorca is that of the **Moros i Cristians**. Although it is celebrated in various coastal villages, its script is always similar. In Sóller a villager representing a heroic figure from the past calls the people to the defence of the port against the attacking Moors. The ensuing battle is noisy and colourful, and there is no need to tell you who wins. The procession of Moors and Christians in Pollença is equally impressive.

Another strictly Mallorcan celebration is that of the **Carro de la Beata**. The procession is held in

Palma, Santa Margalida and Valldemossa. In each, a small girl is chosen to represent Mallorca's only saint, Santa Catalina Tomás. Dressed in traditional peasant dress, she is carried through the streets accompanied by traditional music and floats.

By comparison, Palma's **Festa de l'Estandart**, the celebration of the conquest of Mallorca by Jaume I, is quite tame. Held each year on the last day of December, it consists of a flag-carrying procession from the City Hall to the Cathedral by local politicians . A touch of colour is added by uniformed mace bearers, a marching band and mounted police.

A few days later, on the 12th day of Christmas, the **Reyes Magos** (the Three Kings) bring presents to children all over Spain. On the evening of 5 January, they arrive by boat at the fishing port in front of Palma's Sa Llotja. At the water's edge, they mount horses and lead a parade of youngsters through the streets.

Also in Palma and other seaside villages, the fishermen celebrate the days of the **Verge del Carme**, and of **Sant Pere** (16 July and 29 June, respectively) with a boat procession. The festival is attended by the families of the fishermen.

Romerias are village excursions to hermitages – attended as much for the pleasures of dancing and feasting as for their religious importance.

Lent is celebrated in Palma much as it is in most parts of the world – with a carnival. **Sa Rua**, reinstated in Palma since the return of the democracy, attracts thousands of revellers to the last party before Easter. Easter itself is the most celebrated festival in Spain. In Mallorca processions wind through the streets of most towns. Good Friday is the most imp special ortant day and has retained its character for hundreds of years. The **Davallament** in Pollença represents the bringing of Christ's body down from Calvary.

The City of Palma Art Exposition is sponsored by the City Hall, with winners awarded large prizes.

Youngster guarding costumes of the 'cavallets'

Easter parade

Bicycle Day: a cycle tour of Palma (around the 20th).

VILLAGE FESTIVALS:
5, Palma: Cabalgata de los Reyes Magos.
16–17, Palma: Sant Antoni Abat: Animal Parade.
19–20, Palma: Festa de Sant Sebastià; week of fiestas staged in different squares in the town.

February

International Organ Week: organ concerts are held in churches around Palma.

VILLAGE FESTIVAL:
Sunday before Lent, Palma: Sa Rúa; pre-Lent Carnival.

March

Festival of Classical Music: Palma.
Opera Season (March–June): Teatre Principal, Palma.

VILLAGE FESTIVALS:
Holy Week, Palma and villages: winding, costumed processions are held through the streets.
Good Friday, Pollença: El Davallament at El Calvari.

April

International Floating Boat Show: long weekend at the end of April, Poniente Quay, Palma.

VILLAGE FESTIVAL:
Alaró: Romeria al Castell de Alaró.

April/May

Cooking Exhibition: Mostra de Cuina.

May

Fira del Llibre: book fair, Palma.

VILLAGE FESTIVAL:
Port de Sóller: Festa of the patron saint and mock battles between Moors and Christians.

June

Encounter of the Music Bands of Mallorca: throughout June.

VILLAGE FESTIVAL:
Artá: Sant Antoni dance festival.

July

Music Festival of Artá: classical music Sundays 1 July–5/6 August. Info: Town Hall, Artá, tel: 971 83 50 17.
Pollença Festival of Classical Music: July and August in Cloister of Sant Domingo of Pollença. Info: Tourist Office, tel: 971 86 54 67.
Deià Festival: classical music, July and August at the parish church and in Son Marroig, Deià. Info: Mrs Stefani Shepherd, tel: 971 63 91 78.
Serenates d'Estiu: July and August, various buildings in Capdepera. Info: Tourist Office, tel: 971 56 30 33.
Serenates d'Estiu: classical music, once a week in July and August in Bellver Castle, Palma. Info: Joventuts Musicals, tel: 971 71 24 89.

Mediterranean Folk Groups: a few days in July in Parc de la Mar, Palma. Info: Tourist Office, Palma, tel: 971 71 15 27.

Choral Concert – Torrent de Pareis: mid-July, Escorca. Info: Caixa de Baleares 'Sa Nostra', Dept. of Culture, tel: 971 72 52 10.

International Folk Dance Festival: Sóller.

VILLAGE FESTIVALS:
25, Alcúdia: Romeria de la Verge de la Victòria; **Palma**: Verge del Carme.
27–28, Valldemossa: La Beata.

August

Pollença Festival of Classical Music: July, August and September in cloister of Sant Domingo of Pollença. Info: Tourist Office, Port de Pollença, tel: 971 86 54 67.

Concerts on the Grass: classical music, every Saturday in August, Golf Club of Bendinat. Info: Bendinat Golf Club, tel: 971 40 52 00.

Frédéric Chopin Festival: classical music, every Sunday of month in Cartoixa of Valldemossa. Info: Cell Museum, Frédéric Chopin in the Cloister, tel: 971 61 21 06.

Pollença Painting Competition. Info: Tourist Office, tel: 971 86 54 67..

HRH Princess Elena Horse Jumping Trophy: 11 and 12 August in Horse Riding Club School, Bunyola, Palma–Sóller road km12.

VILLAGE FESTIVALS:
2, Pollença: Festa de Ntra. Sra. dels Angels; 'Es Firó' (Moros i Cristians).
24, Montuíri: Festes de Sant Bartomeu (*cossier* dancers).
19–28, Felanitx: Festa de Sant Agustí; **Sóller**: Muestra Internacional Folklórica (folk dancing).
International Music Festival of Cura: weekly concerts. Info: Mrs Antonia Sitjar, tel: 971 20 50 26.

September

Pollença Festival of Classical Music: Cloister of Sant Domingo of Pollença. Info: Tourist Office, Port de Pollença, tel: 971 86 54 67.

Bunyola Festival: classical music in church of Sant Mateu, Bunyola.

VILLAGE FESTIVALS:
First Sunday, Sta. Margalida: Processió de la Beata.
Last Sunday, Binissalem: Festa des Vermar (wine festival).

October

A week of **Historic Organ Concerts**: Palma and Mallorca.

VILLAGE FESTIVAL:
Palma: Fiesta de La Beateta.

November

Andrés Segovia International Guitar Contest: Palma.
Jazz Festival: Palma.
Competition of Infant Choirs of Mallorca, Porto Cristo.

VILLAGE FESTIVAL:
Inca: Dijous Bó (street market)

December

Mallorcan Choruses: Christmas carols, Palma.
VILLAGE FESTIVAL:
31, Palma: Festa de l'Estandart (national celebration commemorating the Christian conquest) with a procession from the Town Hall to the cathedral.

PRACTICAL information

TRAVEL ESSENTIALS

When to Visit

Summer is the traditional time to visit Mallorca but the high season implies crowded beaches, hot, sticky days and queues at the most popular places. The local government is trying to promote off-season tourism and, with some reservations, it makes sense.

A good time to go is in mid-autumn, when the sky is a deep blue and the low

Golondrina tour boat

season prices have begun. The nights are cool enough for a jacket, but the days are still warm.

A still better option is spring, a month or two after the end of the winter rains (the weather in January and February is a bit uncertain). Since a decade-long drought seriously affected the quality of tap water, spring has become the best time for finding full reservoirs and truly fresh water.

Visas and Passports

Mallorca has never been a difficult place to enter. (The newspapers daily report the arrival of everyone from British hooligans to drug kings.)

Visitors from EU countries require only a valid National Identity Card from their home country to enter Spain, as do citizens of Andorra, Austria, Liechtenstein, Monaco and Switzerland.

US citizens, Australians and New Zealanders require a valid passport and are automatically authorised for a three-month stay, which can be renewed for another three months. Visitors from other countries must obtain a visa from the Spanish Consulate in their own country.

Clothing

A note, not so much on what to wear, but where to wear it. Topless is for the beach only. The minimum of a T-shirt and shorts is respectful dress for the city. For churches, a little more more should be worn (cover your shoulders and knees).

Electricity

Almost all of Mallorca has converted to 220 volts AC. Some old hotels may still have a plug or two at 125, but it is unlikely. British 240-volt appliances work perfectly well in Spanish wall plugs, but will need an adaptor.

Climate

Mallorca has suffered an unusual drought during the past decade. The averages therefore are only that — averages. Temperatures in the hottest month, July, range from a high of 33.3°C (91.5°F) to a low of 17.7°C (63.8°F). The coldest month, February, has a statistical high of 14.9°C (58.8°F), and a low of 3°C (37.4°F). But, needless to say, from time to time the thermometer records extremes above and below the averages.

There are inevitably short, heavy rains around the beginning of September, brought on by what is locally called a *gota fría*. The annual rains, if they're on schedule, come in January and February and sometimes even in March. Air-conditioning is becoming the norm in hotels and taxis.

The main pier in Porto Cristo

Local Time

Mallorca is 2 hours ahead of GMT in the summer and 1 hour ahead in the winter.

MONEY MATTERS

One and two peseta coins are now so tiny that they have been labelled the 'dandruff in your pocket'. But the mint is reluctant to get rid of the coins, no doubt because they represent Spain's most basic units of currency. At the same time they haven't come up with bills larger than the 10,000 peseta note, which seems to buy what a 1,000 peseta note did a few years ago. In between are the five (the *duro*), the 10, the 25, the 50, the 100, the 200, and of late the 500 peseta coins. The paper notes which you are still likely to see start at 1,000 pesetas and climb to 2,000, 5,000, and up to the 10,000 peseta note.

Changing money is big business in Mallorca and if you're changing large sums it is worth shopping around. But for small amounts the differences are slight and some of the better rates advertised on the boards outside the offices may be yesterday's. As in most places, travellers' cheques gain a more favourable rate. Credit cards have caught on in touristic Mallorca as if they had been invented there.

Banks are open 9am–1pm Monday–Saturday, to 1.30pm in the winter. In summer they close on Saturday. Savings banks (*Cajas*) open additional hours on Thursdays, from 4.45–7pm. Many banks have streetside 'cash points'. Some will accept Visa cards. Most banks and change bureaux give credit card cash advances but some set a limit of 25,000 pesetas.

Tipping

A normal tip is 10 percent of the bill.

HOW NOT TO OFFEND

As a rule, Mallorcans are fairly easygoing people. There are only three subjects which are better left alone: the Catholic Church, the King and Gibraltar. Although the majority of the population doesn't even go to Mass on a regular basis, Mallorcans will jump on an outside detractor with the intensity of a newly-converted believer if their religion is belittled in any way.

The second subject, the King, is slightly more complex. King Juan Carlos and his family spend their summers in the Cala Mayor Palace of Marivent and the royal family is considered an integral part of the ambience of Mallorca. Although it is hard to find an islander who isn't a devoted fan of the royals (as well as being a genuinely nice person the King is also considered beneficial for the island's tourism), you will find some Mallorcans who are anti-monarchists. Whether it's the King or the tourism his detractors are worried about is hard to say.

The controversial subject of Gibraltar comes and goes. It tends to come when there are no other major crises affecting the lives of the Mallorcans. Be forewarned not to bring up the subject if you believe it should remain part of Great Britain.

Although a great percentage of the younger population is happy to walk the island's beaches topless, total nudity should be kept to specific areas. The example of the German lady walking into the army canteen in Cabrera without so much as a smile on seems really beyond belief, but it's true. A little common sense goes a long way.

WHOM DO YOU TRUST

Today in Mallorca, you can trust anybody whom you would trust back home. As far as crime is concerned, remember to keep your eye on your purse and your camera at all times and don't let the gypsy flower sellers get too close to your pockets.

You are advised to check your change in tourist areas. If you feel you've been 'had' in a bar, check the prices against the list posted on the wall. If there is no list, the owner is already in violation of the law and can be denounced to the corner policeman. If there is no corner policeman, ask for the *Libro de Reclamaciones* (complaints book) and fill out a complaint (the language isn't important but make it out as neatly as possible and put your passport number and name with it). This isn't the waste of time it might seem. The pages are all numbered and are checked by inspectors every few months. If a page is missing, the owner is up to his ears in trouble. If he has a complaint, he is obliged to answer for it or pay a fine or lose his licence. Because this is a rather serious matter for the owner, you should try your best to be as objective as possible about the misdemeanor.

As the number of foreigners interested in buying houses increases, so does the number of crooked lawyers. Housebuying here is a complicated business and requires the same legal attention it does in any country. Listen to the experiences of your fellow countrymen but don't take it as legal advice. Most expatriates on Mallorca still can't read the headlines in the local newspaper, so how can they understand the fine print of a sales contract? There are lots of English-speaking Spanish lawyers around who are willing to help. Your embassy can supply a list of names.

TOURIST INFORMATION

Tourist information is readily available in most parts of Mallorca. In Palma there are three offices: in **Plaça de la Riena 2**, in **Plaça Espanya** and at **carrer de Sant Domingo 11**. There is another one in the **airport**. All these offices can supply information on any part of the island. In the main towns there is nearly always an information office which can help you with the local areas. If you cannot find the closest information office, ask a local for directions to the *Oficina de Información turística*.

971 75 54 40 or 971 40 14 14. There is a surcharge for this, as there is for airport pick up, multiple suitcases, and any other excuse drivers can find to surcharge. The extra charges are listed on a card inside the cab.

The meter rates only apply inside the urban area and the area directly around the city. If you are going outside the capital be sure to ask the price before you set off on the journey. If you are going off into the wilderness to a private house, give the driver a generous tip rather than have a protracted argument. Cabs are good value within Palma but rather expensive for longer distances.

Rent-a-car

Renting cars is expensive. All of the major international agencies are represented and a few others as well. Cars may be rented at the airport or through a travel agent in town. In high season it is often the case that the local rental companies will not consider renting for periods of fewer than three or four days.

The most popular vehicle at the moment is the Suzuki jeep, but even if you have a four-wheel drive, we suggest you stick to the roads and leave nature to the hikers.

Be forewarned that parking laws are enforced by the ORA in Palma and other urban centres. Tickets can be bought at the *tobacos* shops or in nearby machines. As it is more difficult to collect fines from tourists, there is a tendency to tow away rental cars first.

Boat

Besides the dozens of boat excursions listed in the tourist pamphlet *Excursiones en Barca – Boat Tours*, which details the itineraries of the *golondrina* (swallow) tour boats, there are regular car and passenger ferries sailing to Barcelona and Valencia as well as to the other Balearic islands. High speed trips on a hydrofoil boat to Ibiza are also available from the same company, the Trasmediterránea (tel: 971 70 23 00), and from Flebasa (tel: 971 4053 60). Flebasa also runs a fast twin-hulled catamaran out of Alcúdia to both Ciutadella in Menorca and to a small port near Barcelona. On a calm

GETTING AROUND

Bus

There are several bus companies in Mallorca travelling to virtually every point on the island. In general, they leave Palma from the area around **Plaça Espanya** and the **Rambla**. The information office (tel: 971 75 34 45) in the same square has a detailed folder outlining the routes. The folder is appropriately called *BUS*.

There are two bus companies running in Palma. The first operates the city buses which are painted blue and white and are cheaper, but don't go to the outlying tourist areas such as Palma Nova and Magaluf. There are complicated route maps near all the blue bus stops. If you plan to use this bus line a lot it is worth buying a ten-trip *Bonobus* at one of the 'Caixa' banks. Two punches of this multi-use ticket will get you to the airport.

The cream and red PLAYA-SOL buses of the other bus company can be identified by the logo of a rising sun. The stops are usually close to the city bus stops. These buses will not pick up passengers within the city limits on their in-bound journeys.

Bus services between Palma and the rest of the island are usually reduced in winter.

Taxis

The taxis in Palma are all radio controlled and may be ordered by calling

The drivers are all licenced and the majority are friendly and have good intentions, but the details they impart about the historic sites along the way are another thing. Don't take too much of the information as gospel.

Maps

There are numerous maps available. The prettiest is that of the Firestone company, but it contains serious errors. This and other maps are available at newsstands, book stores and hotels.

There are also 'A to Z'-type pocket street atlases of Palma, and another for the villages. They are called *callejeros*. For the extremely interested there is a geographical atlas of the Baleares (*Atlas de Les Illes Balears Ed. Diáfora S.A.*) which covers the geography, economy and history of the islands.

WHERE TO STAY

The Mallorcan tourist office publishes a useful free brochure, *Hotels with Character*. In the following list of recommended hotels, ££££=£150–200, £££=75–150, ££=£50–75, £=25–30.(Prices are per person in a double room: add 15 percent VAT in luxury hotels or 6 percent in others.)

Palma Hotels

BELLVER
Passeig Maritim 11
Tel: 971 28 99 62
££
Located downtown but nevertheless quiet. Two swimming pools, pleasant garden, restaurant and cafeteria.

BORN
carrer Sant Jaume 3
Tel: 971 71 29 42
£
Tastefully renovated palace, in the city centre. No restaurant, but breakfast is served in the cafeteria or on the lovely patio. A real gem.

GRAN HOTEL SON NET
Castillo Son Net, Puigpunyent (15 minutes from Palma centre)
Tel: 971 14 70 01

day, the trip to Menorca is worthwhile just for the excursion. Tickets and reservations for both companies can be purchased at any travel agency or from the port.

Airlines

Thanks to tourism, the airport of Palma is the second busiest airport in Spain. In any one day in the summer, aircraft from at least 30 countries can be seen. Mallorca may be the best connected place in Europe.

Getting on the flights is another thing altogether. Since there is absolutely no economic advantage to going directly to the airline office, we suggest you let a travel agent earn his commission by searching for and booking your flight. Be forewarned; although there are hundreds of aircraft arriving and leaving every day, you must book in advance. It is not uncommon to discover that the weekend you want to go to Barcelona, for example, is completely booked up (including the boat).

Trains

As well as the famous 'train to Sóller', which runs four trips between **Palma** and **Sóller** every day (plus another tourist trip), there is a train leaving from Palma's **Plaça d'Espanya** towards **Inca**. A commuter train, it leaves both the island capital and Inca about once every hour, with extra trains at rush hours. It stops at **Santa María**, **Consell** and **Binissalem** along the way.

Horse Carts

At various sites in Palma and in other tourist centres there are ranks of horse drawn *galeras* waiting to whisk you off on a romantic tour of the old city. The prices are fixed for the cart, which holds four passengers. The tour of the old city takes about an hour.

Centrally located. Restaurant and cafeteria, salon and television lounge.

VALPARAISO PALACE
Francisco Vidal Sureda, s/n
Tel: 971 40 04 11
Fax: 971 40 59 04
£££
Indoor and outdoor pool, sauna, tennis, boutique, jeweller. A variety of restaurants and bars. And a magnificent view.

HEALTH AND EMERGENCIES

The Water

If you can get past the taste of Mallorca's tap water, it is fit to drink. Because of ten years of drought, much of the local water is high in salinity. Its taste varies drastically from town to town and even from neighbourhood to neighbourhood within Palma. Consequently, the local custom is to drink bottled spring water *con gas* (sparkling) or *sin gas* (still). In all but the worst bars the ice is made with bottled water, as is the coffee.

If you come down with a bad stomach, a pharmacy can give you something for it without a prescription. Hours of *farmacias* are 9.30am–1.30pm and 5–8pm. If the nearest one isn't open, there will be a list of the 'duty pharmacies' posted.

Jot down the street, ask a local, and if he indicates that it is complicated to get to, take a taxi.

Fax: 971 14 70 01
££££
Small and peaceful luxury hotel, in a grand 17th-century *finca*, with a magnificent swimming pool and excellent restaurant overlooking the Tramuntana mountains.

HOSTAL-RESIDENTIA PONS
Calle Vi 8
Tel: 971 72 26 58
£
Simple but clean rooms in a charming centrally located old building with a courtyard full of plants.

PALACIO CA SA GALESA
carrer de Miramar 8
Tel: 971 71 54 00
Fax: 971 72 15 79
££££
Small exclusive British-owned hotel in a restored *palacio* in the heart of medieval Palma. Brilliant views of the cathedral and Palma Bay from the roof terrace. Don't miss tea-time in Monet's Yellow Kitchen.

SAN LORENZO
carrer Sant Llorenç 14
Tel: 971 72 82 00
££–£££
Six rooms in a lovingly restored 17th-century mansion in old Palma, with rooftop swimming pool.

SOL JAIME III
Passeig Mallorca 14B
Tel: 971 72 58 43
Fax: 971 72 59 46
££

Other

Use a high factor sunscreen, especially during the summer, and try to avoid the midday sun. Anti-diarrhoea pills can come in handy, as can mosquito repellent.

Ambulances

Palma, tel: 971 20 41 11.
Andratx, tel: 971 67 27 67.
Felanitx, tel: 971 58 21 12.
Inca, tel: 971 50 45 15.
Manacor, tel: 971 55 40 75.
Pollença, tel: 971 53 34 63.
Sóller, tel: 971 63 34 42.

Hospitals and First Aid Stations

In Mallorca, first aid is never far away. Many villages have first aid stations or hospitals. If they are not easily found, ask someone for the *Casa de Socorro* or the *Cruz Roja* (Red Cross; tel: 971 29 50 00).

Hospitals in Palma

The Social Security Hospital will attend to injured visitors free of charge. You will be asked for some equivalent social health identification from your home country (in Britain form E111, available from post offices). The **social security hospital** is **Hospital Son Dureta**, carrer Andrea Doria 55, Palma, tel: 971 28 91 00. The provincial government supports a **public hospital**, the **Hospital General**, Plaça del Hospital 3, Palma, tel: 971 72 38 06 or 971 71 00 48. A **private clinic** which is popular amongst visitors because of its staff's abilities in various languages is the **Clínica Femenia, S.A.**, carrer Camilo José Cela 20, Palma, tel: 971 45 23 23.

Emergency Doctor

A doctor is available 24 hours a day at **Hospitalización Urgencias Médicas**, carrer Gabriel A. Villalonga 22, Palma, tel: 971 72 22 22.

Emergency Dentist

There are no dentists on permanent call. In case of emergency call the 'emergency doctor' listed above and they will arrange for the appropriate dentist.

Police Emergencies

The police emergency number is 091.

Mallorca seems to be awash with policemen. That is, of course, until you need one. They come dressed in various uniforms. Those dressed in black and white are the Policía Nacional, who are in charge of most things. They have their headquarters at carrer **Ruiz de Alda 8** (tel: 971 28 04 00). They drive large Citroën cars painted black and white with a Spanish flag incorporated into the design. The Policía Municipal in Palma drive blue and white cars marked with either 'Local Police' or 'Metropolitan Police'. They are responsible for the traffic and other specifically urban problems. The Guardia Civil are still dressed in their traditional dark green, but have got rid of the *tricornio* hat which was

their most identifiable feature for decades. They now have jurisdiction only in rural areas and are most often seen executing traffic duties along the highways.

Palma has as well its 'Port Police' who are dressed in grey, 'parking control police' in blue and the 'port parking control police' in still another colour. And, of course, 'tourist police' are found in high-density areas in the summer.

If you are robbed on the street tell the nearest one. If you have lost something which the insurance company is going to have to pay for, you will have to go to the Policía Nacional headquarters to make an official *denouncement*.

Mail and Messages

The **Post Office**, the *Correos*, is located in Palma on the right-hand side of **carrer Constitució**, off the city's main promenade, the **Passeig del Born**. Stamps are bought in the basement. To send a registered letter the stamps and the certification paper must be bought in the basement and filled out before turning them in to one of the certified windows on the main floor. Postal giros are also sent from the street level floor. On the second floor you can send and receive telegrams.

The main post office is open Monday–Friday 8.30am–8.30pm, Saturday 9.30am–2pm; you can send or receive telegrams 24 hours a day.

There are only three branch post offices in Palma. One is near Plaça Espanya, on **carrer O. Perelló**. Another is located on **carrer Anibal** near Plaça Progrés. And in El Terreno, the third one is on **Avinguda Joan Miró** near the turn to Can Barbará. Hours are 9am–1pm.

If you already know the stamps needed for your letter you can buy them at the *estancos*, which are easily identifiable by their maroon and yellow *Tabacos* sign over the door. The owners can generally help you with the stamps you need for postcards and letters back home.

To send anything from registered letters to large packages you will be well looked after at **L'expenditiva** on **carrer Soledad**, beside the main post office.

A fax can be sent from **Telefon CCC**, carrer Sant Miquel 42, and from some travel agents (look for fax signs outside) and a growing number of stationers.

Telephone Calls

Telephone calls can be made in almost any bar. Most have either a phone with

a meter, which can be used for local calls and paid for by the *pasos*, or a green phone which accepts as much money as you want to load in and, in theory, returns unused coins.

Public telephone boxes have gravity-feed phones. Line up the coins you think you will need for the call and they will drop into the phone as it demands more money. Many public phones now take a phonecard (*Crediphone*) which can be bought from post offices and *tabacos*. Rates are cheaper between 10pm and 8am.

To phone a foreign country, dial 07, wait for a new continuous tone, and dial the country code, the area code and then the number. To call within Spain, first dial the area code (91 for Madrid, for example) then the number. To call within Mallorca, Ibiza and Menorca, you now need to dial 971 before the number.

In Palma, the central telephone office is located near the main post office at the corner of **carrer Constitució** and the **Passeig del Born**.

Shipping

If you don't speak Catalan or Spanish, we suggest you make your shipping enquiries through Frank Short at **Avinguda Antoni Maura 26A**. If you are competent to do business in either of the two local languages then the Yellow Pages are full of reputable alternatives, listed under *Transportes*.

The News Media

Since the death of Franco the news media has had a 'boom town' mentality. At first, new newspapers and magazines appeared almost daily and closed just as fast. Happily, most of those which began as worthwhile projects have endured. But there is still an avalanche of choices. The major city newspapers from all over Spain are available. The national papers produced in the EU countries arrive daily.

In addition, Mallorca has five daily newspapers all hitting the streets seven days a week. The local English-language newspaper is the *Majorca Daily Bulletin*, which gives too little local news scattered among the 'back home' news from Britain. The glossy bilingual magazine *Balearic Homes and Living* is also available, with an up-market image of the island.

The local radio has one station broadcasting in English at 103.2 on the FM band. And at 2pm every day on the second TV channel is the British news, followed by an extremely brief comment on the Spanish news in English.

For long-term visitors, TV3, broadcast from Barcelona in the Catalan language, has a converter for listening to the transmitted movies in their original versions. And as may be expected, many hotels and bars now receive satellite TV and the bars normally tune in the stations requested by the majority of their clients.

USEFUL INFORMATION

Business Hours

In Mallorca the hours still revolve around the ancient Spanish custom of the *siesta*. The idea began as a way of surviving the hottest hours of the day by sleeping. But with Spain becoming an integral part of Europe the need to modernise has, in some cases, overcome tradition.

Shops normally open in the morning at 9.30am, close for lunch at 1.30pm, reopen again at 4.30 or 5pm and stay open until 8 or 8.30pm. They are also open on Saturday mornings. The Post Office and Iberia Airlines office also fall into this category. Supermarkets such as **Pryca** and **Continente** and some department stores (*galerias preciados*) are open over lunch hour, longer into the evening and all day Saturday. Prior to Christmas most of the stores, big and small, extend their hours to catch the holiday trade. The private sector companies, such as insurance companies, follow basically the same hours in winter but work only an extended morning in the summer, weekdays only.

Banks are only open in the mornings from 9am until 1pm, Monday to Saturday. Savings banks, called *cajas d'ahorro*, usually have slightly longer hours. Both types are closed Saturday in summer. Government offices and institutions are normally open on weekday mornings only.

Public Holidays

In Mallorca, any list of public holidays may be valid only for the present calendar year. Autonomous politics is causing the Mallorcans to stop celebrating some Spanish fiestas in favour of others considered of more local interest.

In Mallorca, as in all Roman Catholic countries, each day is dedicated to one or more saints. The important 'saints' days' have become public holidays. For a Mallorcan, celebrating your 'saint's day' is just as important as celebrating your birthday.

Market Days

Monday Morning: Calviá; Lloret; Manacor; Montuíri.
Tuesday Morning: Alcúdia; Artá; Campanet; Llubí; Porreres; Santa Margarita; **Tuesday Afternoon**: Ca'n Picafort.
Wednesday Morning: Andratx; Capdepera; Colonia St. Jordi; Llucmajor; Port de Pollença; Selva; Sencelles; Sineu.
Thursday Morning: Ariany; Campos; El Arenal; Inca; Sant Llorenç; Ses Salines.

Friday Morning: Algaida; Binissalem; María de la Salut; Pont d'Inca; Santa Eugnia; Son Servera; **Friday Afternoon**: Alaró.
Saturday Morning: Buger; Bunyola; Cala Ratjada; Campos Costitx; Lloseta; Palma; Santa Margalida; Santanyí; Sóller.
Sunday Morning: Alcúdia; Llucmajor; Muro; Pollença; Sa Pobla; Santa María.

GOLF

For further information call the **Federació Balear de Golf,** Palma, tel: 971 72 27 53, fax: 971 71 17 31.

Competitions

Balearic Championships (second week in February).
International Open of the Baleares (March).
Baleares International Championship (Santa Ponça; April).
Pollença Golf Club Trophy (April).
HRH Conde de Barcelona Challenge (May).
Balearic Islands Trophy (June).
Spanish Professional Championship (September).
Baleares Golf Federation Prize (September).
Island of Mallorca Trophy (telephone for information).

Golf Clubs

REAL GOLF DE BENDINAT: men's and women's amateur tees; nine hole, par 68; 7kms (4.3 miles) from Palma on the road to Andratx in the Bendinat housing estate. Tel: 971 40 52 00.
GOLF POLLENÇA: men's and women's amateur and professional tees; nine hole, par 72; 49.3kms (30.6 miles) from Palma, 3kms (1.9 miles) from Pollença. Tel: 971 53 32 16.
GOLF PONIENT: men's and women's amateur and professional tees; 18 hole, par 72; 18kms (11 miles) from Palma on the crta. to Cala Figuera. Tel: 971 13 01 48.
GOLF SANTA PONÇA: men's and women's amateur and professional tees; 18 hole, par 72; 18kms (11 miles) from Palma. Tel: 971 69 02 11.

CANYAMEL GOLF CLUB: 18 hole, par 72; 76kms (47 miles) from Palma near Capdepera. Tel: 971 56 44 57.

CLUB DE GOLF SON SERVERA: men's and women's amateur and professional tees; nine hole, par 72; 68kms (42 miles) from Palma near the Costa de los Pinos. Tel: 971 56 78 02.

SON VIDA GOLF: men's and women's amateur and professional tees; 18 hole, par 72; on the outskirts of Palma in the Son Vida development. Tel: 971 79 12 10.

VALL D'OR GOLF CLUB: men's professional and women's amateur tees; nine hole, par 70; 59kms (33.6 miles) from Palma, at km7.7 on the road from Porto Colom to Cala D'Or. 971 83 70 01.

SAILING

For further information call the **National Sailing School,** Cala Nova, at 971 40 25 12.

Competitions

Mare Nostrum Trophy: Snipe, 420, TCV (February).
HRH Princess Sofia Trophy (Easter week).
European Championships of FD (July).
Mallorca Trophy (July).
The King's Cup (August).
Adm. Conde de Barcelona Trophy: epoch boats (August).
Calviá Coast Trophy (September).
Hispanity Regatta (October).

THE LANGUAGE

Any visitor to Mallorca without a Catalan dictionary may run into problems. Along with Spanish, Catalan is the official language here.

Street signs in Spanish are being replaced almost daily by signs in Catalan. This language is also a required subject in those schools where all subjects are not already being taught in Catalan.

This creates problems for visitors, whose lives are complex enough without having to read a city map saying *Catedral* for the Cathedral while following street signs saying *Seu*.

The transition to Catalan would be more tolerable if it weren't for the pol-

itics involved. New direction signs have sprung up all over the island indicating various points of touristic or other interest. The signs, as one can imagine, are in Catalan with pictographs. Since the Mallorcans don't need the directions and the tourists can only read the diagrams, then who are the signs for? You guessed it! They're to let the Spaniards from the peninsula know that Spanish is not the language spoken here. The rector of the local university is quoted as saying, 'Mallorca is a bilingual island – Catalan and English'.

But even though you may not understand a word spoken in the cafés, your high school Spanish will work. In the urban areas there is no one who doesn't speak Castilian.

Throughout ths book, we have tried to give you the Catalan version of the place name. Some words are similar, while others, such as that for cathedral, are completely unrelated.

Words you will see in this book:

MEANING	CASTILIAN	CATALAN
Arch	Arco	Arc
Avenue	Avenida	Avinguda
Baths	Baños	Banys
Bay	bahia	badia
Cathedral	Catedral	Seu
City Hall	Ayuntamiento	
		Ajuntament
Museum	Museo	Museu
Palace	Palacio	Palau
Palma	Palma	Ciutat
Park	Parque	Parc
Promenade	Paseo	Passeig
Quay	Muelle	Moll
Square	Plaza	Plaáa
Street	calle	carrer
Theatre	Teatro	Teatre
Village	pueblo	pobla
Welcome	bienvenido	benvinguts

When it comes to more mundane parts of speech such as greetings, the differences become even greater and arrive at the point where they are totally impenetrable to those who don't speak the language. Even though there are similarities because they are both Romance languages, Català is a language by itself. It is *NOT* a dialect of Castilian. *Bona Sort!*

Index

A

Ajuntament (Palma) 25
Alaró 45, 51, 67
Albufera 37, 72
Alcúdia 37, 71–2, 82, 86, 93
Alfábia 29, 50
Alfons III 16
Algaida 47, 87, 88, 96
Almacenes Aguila (Palma) 25
almonds 16, 42, 67
Almudaina Palace (Palma) see Palau de
    l'Almudaina
'alpargatería' 94
Andratx 38, 39
antiques 51, 91–2
Aquacity 63
Arabs see Moors
Aragón, Kingdom of 12, 16
Arc de l'Almudaina (Palma) 25
Arc de la Drassana Reial (Arco de la
    Ataranza Real) (Palma) 28, 55
Archduke Luis Salvador 30–1, 32, 57
art 42, 46, 53, 55, 58, 71, 74, 92–3
Artá 73, 75, 98
Auto Safari 76

B

Baleares islands 10–12, 16
banks 101, 109
Banyalbufar 40, 58
Banys Arabs (Arab baths) (Palma) 23,
    55

Barceló, Antoni 13
Barcelona 38, 108
Bardolet, Coll 32, 57, 58
Bayeu, Fray Manuel 58
beaches 43, 64, 72, 75
Bellini, Eduardo 35
Bellver Castle see Castell del Bellver
Bendinat Castle 37
Biniamar 67
Binissalem 33, 51–2, 71, 91, 99, 104
Blauets Choir 49
Blitz, Gérard 78
boat tours 38, 60, 104
'bordados' (crochet) 89
Bunyola 29, 59, 65, 87, 99
Burwitz, Nils 32, 52, 57
buses 103
Byzantines 11, 16

C

Ca la Torre (Palma) 23
Ca'n Picafort 73
Cabrera archipelago 64
cafés 80–1
Caimari 41, 68
Caixa de Barcelona (Palma) 26, 93
Cal Rei 66
Cala Blava 63
Cala Bona 75
Cala d'Or 77, 78, 84
Cala Estellencs 38, 39
Cala Figuera 36, 78
Cala Figuera (Calviá) 82

Cala Llonga (Cala d'Or) 78
Cala Marçal 77
Cala Marmassen 38
Cala Millor 75
Cala Mondragó 78
Cala Murada 77
Cala Portals Vells 44
Cala Ratjada 74
Cala Romantica 77
Cala Tuent 41, 60
Calas de Mallorca 77
Caldentey, Pere 76
'caldereta de llagosta' 35
California 13, 16, 24, 54
Calonge 44, 45, 77
Calvari (Pollença) see El Calvari
Calviá 70
Camp de Mar 37
Campanet 33
Campos 44, 64, 78
Can Alomar (Muro) 52
Can Ayamans (Lloseta) 67
Can Berga (Palma) 26
Can Bordils (Palma) 25
Can Capità Flexes (Palma) 27
Can Cal.lar del Llorer (Palma) 24
Can Chacón (Palma) 27
Can Conrado (Santa Maria) 51
Can Formiguera (Palma) 23
Can Garriga (Binissalem) 52
Can Garriga (Sineu) 53
Can Gelabert (Binissalem) 52
Can Joan de S'Aigua (Palma) 24
Can Llull (Palma) 27
Can Malonda (Palma) 23
Can March (Cala Ratjada) 74
Can Montenegro (Palma) 27
Can Moragues (Palma) 23
Can Oleo (Palma) 25
Can Oleza (Palma) 24
Can Oms (Palma) 25
Can Prunera (Soller) 60
Can Quint (Palma) 27
Can Rei (Palma) 25
Can Sollerich (Palma) 27, 93
Can Toro (Alcúdia) 71

Can Vivot (Palma) 22
Can Zavellá (Palma) 24
Cap Andritxol 37
Cap Blanc 63
Cap d'es Pinar 37
Cap Ferrutx 37, 73
Cap Formentor 33, 36–7, 48
Cap Freu 37
Cap Llamp 37
Capdepera 75, 98
Capocorb Vell 63, 64
carnival 97–8
Carro de la Beata 97
Carthaginians 11, 16
Cartoixa (Valldemossa) see Real
  Cartoixa de Jesus de Nazaret
Casa Blanca 62, 87
Casa Casasayas (Palma) 26
Casa de l'Almoina (Palma) 28
Casa del Marques de Palmer 22, 23
Casa Juliá (Palma) 23
Cases Velles de Formentor 36
Castell d'Alaró 66, 98
Castell de Bellver 12, 56, 70
Castell de Capdepera 75
Castell de Sant Telm 38
Castell de Santueri 45
Català (language) 8, 14, 108, 110–11
Catalans 11, 12, 13, 14, 55, 75, 99
Cathedral (Palma) 22, 28, 56
'cavallets' 96, 97
Centro Arqueológico Hispano-
  Americano (Alcúdia) 71
Centro Cultural de la Misericordia
  (Palma) 93
Chopin, Frederick 31, 57, 58, 99
churches
  Capella de Nostra Senyora de la
    Esperansa (Capdepera) 75
  Capella de Santa Ana (Palma) 55
  Capella del Sant Cristo (Alcudia) 71
  Montesió (Palma) 23
  Nostra Senyora del Carme (Porto
    Cristo) 76
  Nostra Senyora dels Angels
    (Pollença) 35

Sant Antoniet (Palma) 25
Sant Bartomeu (Valldemossa) 58
Sant Jaume (Alcúdia) 37, 71
Sant Jaume (Porto Colom) 77
Sant Joan Bautista (Calviá) 70
Sant Joan Bautista (Deiá) 30
Sant Miquel (Palma) 25
Sant Pedro (Petra) 54
Sant Pere Apostòl (Esporlas) 69
Santa Catalina (Palma) 25
Santa María de Sineu 53
Santa María la Mayor (Inca) 41
Transfiguració del Senyor (Artá) 73
Círculo de Bellas Artes 26, 93
climate 11, 100, 101
Club Med 78
Coll de Sóller 29
Colom, Guillem 24
Coloni de Sant Pere 73
Coloni de Sant Jordi 64
Comasema 66
Comellar de sa Cometa Negra 42
concerts 43, 76, 82, 98, 99
Consell 51, 71, 91, 92, 104
Consell Insular de Mallorca 25
Consulat de la Mar (Palma) 27
Convent de Montesió (Pollenca) 37
Convent de Sant Bernadó (Petra) 56
Convent de Sant Domingo (Pollença) 35
Convent de Sant Francesc (Palma) 14, 23
Convent de Santa Clara (Palma) 23
Convent dels Mínims (Santa María) 51
Convent dels Mínims (Muro) 52
Córdoba, Emirate of 12, 16
Cosconar 42
cossiers 96
Costa d'en Blanes 37
Costa de Calviá 70
Costa i Llobera, Miquel 33, 36
Coves d'Artá 75
Coves de Hams 76
Coves de Campanet 33
Coves del Drac 76, 77
Cuculla de Fartáritx 48
Cura see Nostra Senyora de Cura

D

Darío, Rubén 57
Deià 30–1, 58, 87, 98
Denia, Taifa of 16
Desmás, Francesc 39
discos 81–2
Dragonera 38, 60

E

Easter 96–8
Eivissa (Ibiza) 11, 78
El Calvari (Pollença) 33, 48, 98
El Colomer 36
El Portón 81
electricity 101
Embalse de Cúber 49
Embalse del Gorg Blau 49
'ensaimadas' 77, 86, 91
Entreforc 42, 49
Ermita de Betlem 74
Ermita de la Victoria 72
Ermita de Sant Llorenç 43
Ermita de Trinidad 31, 58
Es Capdellá 69, 70
Es Carritxó 45
Es Glop 38
Es Trenc 64
Escorca 48
Esporles 40, 68–9, 89
Establiments 68, 70
Estellencs see Cala Estellencs
exhibitions 26, 27

F

Far de Capdepera 74
Felanitx 44, 44–5, 91, 96, 99
Felipe V 13, 16
Femenia Nou 48
Femenia Vell 48
Ferrer, Jaume 27
Ferrer, Pep Costa 78
festivals 58, 96–9
flamenco 82

Font des Teix 50
footwear 89–90, 94
Formentor peninsula 35–6
Fornalutx 50
Foro de Mallorca 52
Fortuny family 69
Franco, Francisco 14, 16

G

Galatzó 66, 70
Galilea 70
galleries 53, 93
Gaudí, Antoni 28, 42, 49
glass-making 47, 88
golf 109–10
Goya, Francisco 58
Graves, Robert 30
'gregal' (wind) 35

H, I, J

hang-gliding 72
Hapsburgs 12
'honderos' 11, 28
Ibiza see Eivissa
Inca 33, 41, 47, 51, 52, 68, 71, 87, 99,
   104
'indianos' 38
Jaume I 12, 16, 23, 38, 44, 75, 97
Jaume II 12, 16, 38, 57
Jaume III 16

L

L'Ardiacanat (Palma) 28
La Rambla (Palma) 25, 94
language 14–15, 109
Laurens, J B 57
Lent 97
liqueurs 52, 91
'llebeix' (wind) 11
Lloseta 67
Llubí 41
Lluc 41, 42
Lluc Alcari 30

Llucmajor 16, 44, 64, 78
Llull, Ramón 12, 16, 27, 47
L'Ofre 49

M

Magaluf 37, 81, 82
Majorica 91
Mal Pas 72
malvasia' 40
Manacor 76, 90–1
Mancor del Vall 67
March Ordinas, Joan 14, 25, 28
Marivent Palace 102
markets 53, 71, 94, 109
Marratxí 88
Martí, King 57
Massanella 33, 49, 67
Maura, Antoni 14, 27, 57
Menorca 16, 37
Menut i Binifaldó 48
Metelo, Quinto Cecilio 11, 16, 72
Mirador de la Creueta 36
Mirador de Ricard Roca 39
Mirador de Ses Animes 39
Mirador de Ses Barques 50
Mirador del Pujol den Banya 59
Miró, Joan 22
Mola, the (Port d'Andratx) 38
Monasteri de Nostra Senyora de Lluc
   42, 48
money 100–01
Montuíri 46, 96, 99
Moore, Henry 74
Moors 11–12, 16, 50, 55, 75, 77
Morey 73
Moros i Cristians 96, 98
Mortitx 48
Muro 41, 52, 53, 73
Museu de Mallorca 55
Museu Diocesá (Palma) 55
Museu Etnológic de Muro 52
Museu Roma de Pollentia (Alcúdia) 71
museums 37, 47, 49, 51, 52, 54, 55–6,
   58, 69, 71, 75

N

Na Foradada 31
Naples 78
Napoleonic Wars 13, 16
nightlife 76–82
Nostra Senyora de Cura 46, 47, 98
Nostra Senyora del Puig 33, 48

O

olive oil 38, 66
Oratori de Nostra Senyora de la
Consolació 44, 78
Oratori de Sant Honorat 45–6
Oratori de Sant Miquel 33
Oratori de Sant Joan 73
Oratori Sant Feliu (Palma) 27
Orquidea 90–1

P

Paguera 37
Palau de Justicia (Palma) 26
Palau de l'Almudaina 12, 28, 55
Palau de Rei Sanç (Valldemossa) 31,
57, 58
Palau March (Palma) 28
Palma de Mallorca 11, 16, 22–8, 55–6,
59, 70, 78, 86–7, 88, 89, 90, 93–4,
97, 98, 99, 102–3, 104, 105
Palma Nova 37
Palmanyola 65
Parc de la Mar (Palma) 22, 28
pearls, artificial 90–1
Pensión Menorquina (Palma) 26
Penyaflor (Alaró) 66
Pere IV 16
Petra 13, 54
Phoenicians 11, 16
piracy 13, 16, 39
Pla de Palma 62
Plaça Cort (Palma) 25, 94
Plaça Drassanes (Palma) 27
Plaça d'Espanya (Palma) 25, 41, 46,
51, 59, 67, 69, 73

Plaça de Toros (Muro) 53
Plaça Joan Carles I (Palma) 26, 80,
93, 94
Plaça Major (Palma) 25, 94
Plaça Weyler (Palma) 14, 82, 93
Platja de Canyamel 75
police 106
Pollença 33, 34, 35–7, 45, 47, 48,
49, 89, 92, 93, 98, 99
Pollentia 11, 37, 71–2
Pont Romà (Pollença) 35, 47, 48
Porreres 46
Port d'Alcúdia 72
Port d'Andratx 37–8, 81, 87
Port de Pollença 35, 87
Port de Sollér 60
Port des Canonges 40
Porto Colom 75, 77
Porto Cristo 75, 76–7, 98
Porto Petro 78
Portol 88
Posada de Cartoixa (Palma) 23
pottery 88
Pryca 68
Pueblo Español (Palma) 55–6
Puig d'Alaró 66–7
Puig de Ca de Miner 48
Puig de Sa Creu 54
Puig de Randa 46
Puig de Sant Martí 72
Puig Major 33, 49–50
Puig Roig 42, 43, 49
Puig Tomir 33, 48
Puigpunyent 69
Punic Wars 11

R

Randa 46, 47
Real Cartoixa de Jesus de Nazaret
(Valldemossa) 31, 32, 57, 58
restaurants 84–7
'roba de llengues' 51, 89
Rodin, Auguste 74
Romans 11–12, 35
romerias 85, 97, 99

S

S'Alqueria Blanca 44, 45, 78, 92
S'Arracó 38
S'Hort del Rei (Palma) 28
S'Horta 44, 77
Sa Calobra 42, 43, 49, 60
Sa Coma (beach resort) 75
Sa Coma (Valldemossa) 32, 58
Sa Font 38
Sa Granja 40, 69
Sa Llotja (Palma) 27, 56, 78, 93, 97
Sa Pobla 47
Sa Rápita 62, 64
Sa Talaia Moreia 73
Sagrera, Guillem 27
sailing 109
S'Alcadena 66
Salt de la Bella Dona 42
San Francisco 13
Sanç, King 16
Sand, George 31, 57, 58
Sant Jordi 62
Sant Pere 97
Sant Telm 38
Santa Catalina Thomás 31, 54, 58, 57, 61, 96
Santa Margalida 97, 99
Santa Margarita 53
Santa María (del Camí) 33, 47, 51, 71, 89, 91, 93, 104
Santa Ponça 37
Santanyí 44, 78
Santuari de la Consolació see Oratori de Nostra Senyora de la Consolació
Santuari de Bon Any 54
Santuari de Montesió 46
Santuari de Nostra Senyora de Gràcia (Randa) 46
Santuari de Sant Salvador 45–6, 73
S'Estanyol 64
Secar de la Real 68, 69
Selva 41, 42, 68
Serra d'Alfábia 50, 65
Serra de Sant Vicenç 48
Serra de Tramuntana 48, 50, 65
Serra del Cavall Bernat 33
Serra, Fray Junípero 13, 16, 23–4, 54
Ses Carasses (Palma) 27
Ses Coretes 64
Ses Països 73
shopping 41, 51, 88–95
S'Illot 75
Sineu 52, 53, 93
'sirocco' (wind) 11
Sollér 29–30, 42, 49, 50, 59–61, 98, 99, 104
Sollerich 66
Son Angelats 30
Son Berga Nou 68
Son Claret (Calviá) 70
Son Curt 66
Son Ferriol 62
Son Forteza Vell 77
Son Gual (Valldemossa) 58
Son Marroig 30–1, 98
Son Más 39
Son Moragues (Valldemossa) 58
Son Morei Vell 74
Son Perot 66
Son Serra de Marina 73
Son Servera 75
Son Torelló (Sineu) 53
Spanish Civil War 14, 16

T

Talayotic culture 16, 63, 64
taxis 103
Teatre Principal (Palma) 25–6, 82
Teatre Roma (Alcúdia) 37, 72
telephones 107
textiles 40, 51, 69, 88, 89
Torre Cega (gardens) 74
Torre de Canyamel 75
Torrent de Lluc 42, 49
Torrent de Pareis 42, 43, 49, 99
Torrent de Saluet 38
Torrent de Sant Pere 40, 69
Torrent des Gorg Blau 42, 49
Torrent des Guix 42
Tossals 49

trains 25, 59, 73, 104
'tramuntana' (wind) 11
'tramvia' 59, 60

V

Vall de Esporles 68
Vall de Sant Miquel 33
Vall de Superna 69
Vall d'Orient 66
Valldemossa 30–1, 32, 51, 54, 57–8,
    82, 87, 88, 99
Valldurgent 70
Vandals 11, 16

Vilafranca 54
Vilanova (Esporles) 69
Villa Francisca 65
Virgin de Lluc 48
Vistamar (Valldemossa) 58

W,Z

windmills 62
windsurfing 35
wine 13, 16, 40, 51, 52, 77, 91
woodcarving 89
zoos 76
Zupan, Bruno 32, 57

ACKNOWLEDGMENTS

Design concept	**V. Barl**
Cover design	**Klaus Geisler**
Cartography	**Berndtson & Berndtson**
Editorial director	**Dorothy Stannard**